GLASS SOURCE BOOK

GLASS
SOURCE
BOOK

JO MARSHALL

CHARTWELL
BOOKS, INC.

A QUARTO BOOK

Published by Chartwell Books
A Division of Book Sales, Inc.
110 Enterprise Avenue
Secaucus, New Jersey 07094

ISBN 1-55521-637-4

This book was designed and produced by
Quarto Publishing plc
The Old Brewery, 6 Blundell Street
London N7 9BH

Editor: Hazel Harrison
Art Director: Moira Clinch
Assistant Art Director: Chloë Alexander
Picture Manager: Joanna Wiese
Picture Researchers: Arlene Bridewater, David Pratt
Designers: Nick Clark, Daniel Evans, John Grain, Carole Perks, Steven Randall

Typeset by Ampersand Typesetting (Bournemouth) Ltd
Manufactured in Hong Kong by Regent Publishing Services Ltd
Printed in Hong Kong by Leefung Asco Printers Ltd

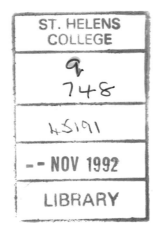

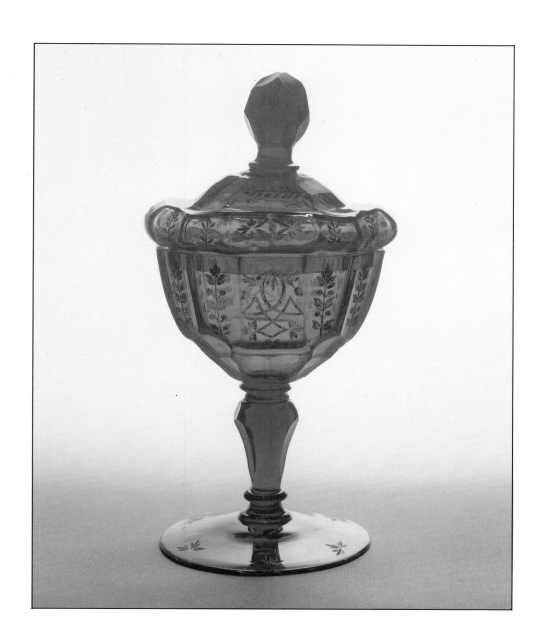

A blue-tinted sweetmeat glass and cover made in Bohemia about 1730.

CONTENTS

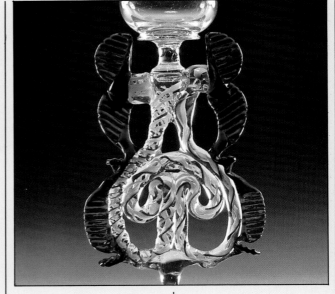

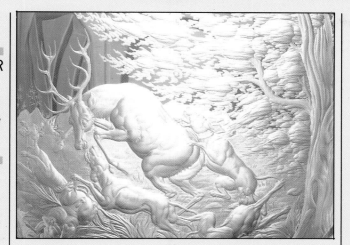

INTRODUCTION

It is only when one tries to imagine a world without glass that one realizes in how many ways it is used and the extent of our unthinking acceptance of it. We all admire the magnificent stained-glass windows in the great cathedrals of the world – which not only added light and a rich overlay of colour to their imposing interiors but also educated the illiterate worshippers with vivid illustrations of stories from the scriptures. But we accept without thought the windows in our houses and offices, and the great modern edifices which are certainly "more glass than wall" – as was once said of the great Elizabethan building, Hardwick House. Those who appreciate the great wines of the world do not necessarily pay much heed to the bottles in which it is stored and the glasses from which it is drunk. And those who are indebted to medical science for diagnostic X-rays and life-giving drugs are not unnaturally unmindful of the widespread use of glass in such things as test tubes, microscopes, medicine bottles, thermometers and X-ray plates. And what of spectacles and electric light bulbs, which give us vision and illumination – not to mention cameras, the cinema and so on.

The raw materials

But these are the products of a sophisticated modern manufacture. The early story of glass is one of slow, gradual discovery. Basically glass is and always has been a product of mere "sand and ashes" (silica and alkali in scientific terms), an artificial compound which can be both translucent and transparent. The sand (or sometimes flint or quartz) provides the silica, and is fused in a furnace at a very high temperature, with the help of an alkaline flux which may be soda or potash.

These are the materials which have continued in use ever since glass was first made, although there have been changes in the kinds of silica and alkali used. The Egyptians and Syrians had no shortage of sand (silica), but the Venetians used white pebbles taken from rivers, while the English from the seventeenth century used calcined and powdered flints. For alkali the Egyptians used natron, but in the Mediterranean area the ash of certain marine plants, which were rich in soda, was used. In Renaissance times this was exported from Spain, and was called barilla. The alkali of potash was obtained from burning bracken or beechwood. Egyptian, Roman (that made throughout the Empire) and Venetian glass was made with soda; English and German glass with potash. Both these are used in present-day commercial glass.

Oxides of lead had been added from early times for colorization, but a glass rich in lead, and therefore ductile, was not made until 1675 when Ravenscroft produced English lead glass. This is brilliant, heavier and softer, and gives a resonant note. The fused or finished

Right *The popular Germanic drinking glass known as a* roemer *comprises a globular bowl, a wide hollow stem embellished with decorative dollops of glass called prunts (which also allow a vessel to be gripped easily) and a foot of threaded or trailed glass. This elegant mid-seventeenth century* roemer *is Netherlandish in origin.*

Below *Early wine bottles assumed a variety of shapes other than the cylindrical bottle in use today, although their colours – like ours today – were mostly greens and browns. These four English examples date from the seventeenth and eighteenth centuries. From left to right are a green bottle stamped "Thomas Carlyon 1708"; a round-ended supine brown vessel from 1630; a squat, bulbous example of opaque glass, and a pale blue bottle from c.1630. Glass wine bottles made their debut in England in the early seventeenth century, replacing the earthenware variety.*

material of all glass is called the metal. In early times the measuring and proportions of the ingredients were sometimes haphazard, giving rise to an excess of alkali. This can result in an unstable or "diseased" glass, as the metal develops a fine network of interior cracks and can eventually decompose and crumble, an effect known in England as crisselling.

Glassmaking techniques

The earliest hollow vessels were either made by the elaborate method called sand core or core wound, or were freely modelled or cast. In the core-winding technique the melted glass was drawn out into threads and wound around a core of sand and clay of the desired shape. This was held on an iron bar, which was used both as a handle and as a "former" for winding threads for the neck of the object. Decoration could be added by pressing into the hot surface threads of coloured glass which could be tooled or combed into a great variety of designs. When cooled, the iron bar contracted and could be easily withdrawn, while the sandy core was removed by scraping; the inner surfaces of these vessels are rough with traces of sand and clay. The casting and moulding methods appear to have immediately preceded glassblowing. In moulding, a sheet or flattened lump of half-molten glass was pressed into the form of a bowl or dish. Some bowls also appear to have been pressed on the outside of a convex mould or core, which may have been of the same sandy clay as that used for the core-wound vessels.

The invention of glassblowing cannot be precisely dated or definitely ascribed to any particular place, but it began to be used in the first half of the first century BC in the countries of the Eastern Mediterranean. With the establishment of the Roman Empire under Augustus (27 BC) the art spread rapidly to Italy and into Gaul. Because it enabled vessels of considerable size to be made, glass could now be used instead of or as well as pottery and metalwork, and glass and glassmaking spread into every province of the Roman Empire.

The tools used in handmade blown glass, like the materials themselves, have continued in use to the present day. Glass is unique as a craftsman's material in that it is worked at a temperature too hot to handle. It is a fluid material – it will stick to an iron blowing tube when wound onto it and withdrawn from the crucible pot. This mass of hot glass, called a gather, is then rolled into a globular or cylindrical mass on an iron marvering table before being blown into a bubble called a paraison. The paraison is manipulated by swinging the tube to elongate it, and is then cut with shears and made into various shapes with tongs and pincers, with the leading craftsman or "gaffer" sitting in a "chair" with long flat arms on which

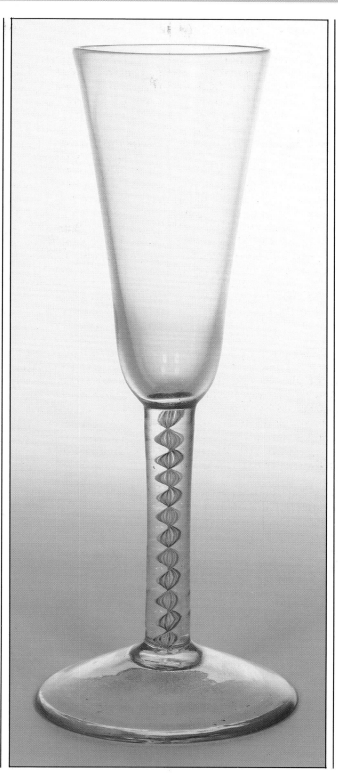

Left *The English ale glass, quite similar in form to the wine glass, developed from the dwarf ale glass of the early 1600s to the later, taller variety, such as this elegant eighteenth-century example. The glass features a stem with a coloured twist, i.e., a spiralled rod of glass. These were an English speciality, and were popular from around 1735 to 1770. Some 150 types of twists and combinations thereof were said to have been made.*

the iron tube or rod is rotated by hand. The glass cools down quickly and must be repeatedly reheated at the furnace, or "glory-hole", to keep its plasticity. This process requires great dexterity, precision and rhythmical movement.

The paraison can also be blown into a mould. Early moulds were made of clay, which was gradually superseded by metal, and at the end of the nineteenth century machinery was made in America to mechanically blow bottles in metal moulds – a similar process to that used for electric light bulbs. Pressed glass, another moulding technique, was also an American invention, and was made from about 1827. A quantity of molten glass is placed into a metal mould which gives the design to the exterior of the vessel, while a plunger gives the shape and desired pattern of the interior, forcing the glass upwards and outwards to fill the entire mould. The method was used originally to produce an expensive imitation of cut glass.

The final stage, for both handblown and machine-made glass, is annealing, or toughening, in a lehr (or leer) chamber or tunnel. This removes the internal strains and stresses, which would otherwise leave the glass brittle and fragile.

A method called lampwork, in which rods and tubes

Left The prime decorative elements on this ornate cut and engraved Bohemian beaker are four polished roundels encircling female figures who represent the Four Elements. The images are taken from engravings by J. de Saadeler after the Antwerp painter Marten de Vos (pictured is Water, or Wasser). The beaker dates from the late seventeenth century.

of glass are heated in the flame of a lamp and pincered, blown and drawn out to the required shape, is used for making small objects such as toys, figures and beads.

Decoration

Methods of decoration fall into two distinct types, the first being integral decoration, which is part of the glassmaking process, as in moulding, the inclusion of coloured glass and the application of glass threads, drops and trailing while the glass is hot.

The second type is where the decoration is added to the finished article, for example painting, gilding, engraving and cutting, the latter done with a lapidary's wheel in imitation of semi-precious stones and rock crystal. Sometimes two or more coloured layers of glass are used, the finest examples of this technique being Roman cameo glass, which required great skill, artistry and immense

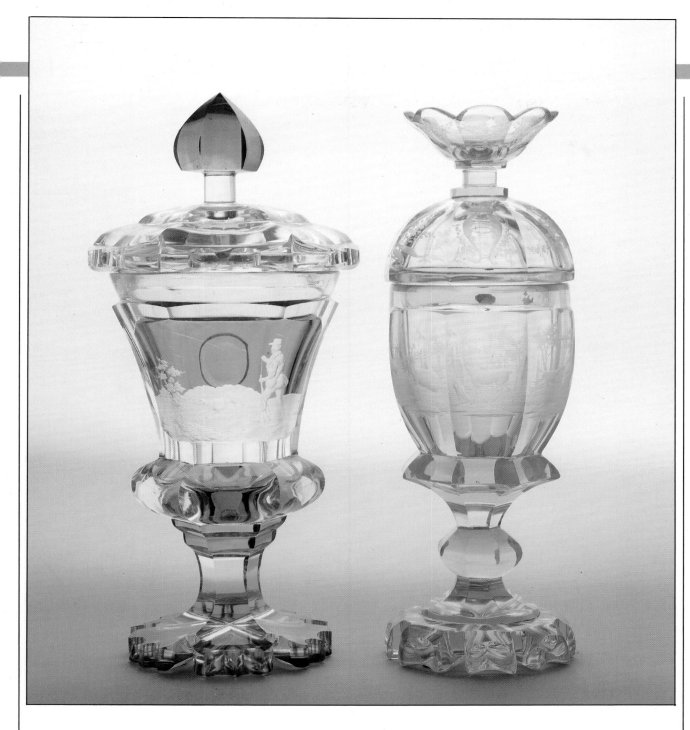

Far left *Although made in Newcastle-upon-Tyne, these two mid-eighteenth-century wine glasses were engraved in Holland, as was much Newcastle glass. The allegorical scene on the glass at left represents Friendship (it reads Vriendschap), and the arms of Holland appear on the slightly taller piece. Both vessels are of the "light baluster" type, which is characterized by multi-knopped stems. Because such large quantities of light balusters were produced in Newcastle, they were also called Newcastle glasses.*

Left *Bohemian glass has a long, esteemed tradition, glass factories having been established in that part of Eastern Europe as early as the fourteenth century. The mid-nineteenth century was a rich era for Bohemian glassmakers, who specialized in ornate engraved glass. The covered goblet (left), made c.1840, bears an engraved design and also has been flashed with a thin layer of amber glass. The ovoid-bowled goblet with cover at right is of a greenish-yellow type known as Annagelb, its colour having been achieved by adding uranium to the batch. Glassmaker Josef Riedel developed Annagelb, as well as the fluorescent yellowish-green Annagrün glass, naming both in honour of his wife.*

patience to produce. Engraving is done with a grindstone-type wheel, using different-sized discs of metal or stone and fed with a stream of abrasive and water. For fine pictorial or decorative engraving a range of smaller copper discs, fed with emery, is used, and the vessel is pressed against the rotating wheel. Vessels of very thin metal, too brittle to withstand wheel-engraving, were often decorated by diamond-point engraving, and in the

Netherlands the diamond was used for elaborate stippled decoration, in which the design is formed by a multitude of tiny dots made by lightly tapping the diamond point into the surface of the glass.

Acid-etching was known in the seventeenth century but little used, and only employed by a minority of glass-makers in the nineteenth. Sand-blasting, in use since 1870, was and is used to produce a copy of a combination

11

Left *Candle chandeliers like this English Rococo example of the eighteenth century were awash in shimmering faceted glass – crystal pendants, undulating arms, even urn-shaped central sections enclosing the metal shaft. Such hanging ceiling fixtures waned in popularity with the introduction of gas lighting in England.*

beautiful glasses. The increasing refinement in eating habits and interest in food and wine required fine glass to adorn the tables, and throughout the eighteenth and nineteenth centuries, with the emergence of a bourgeoisie with money to spend, new markets opened up for glass, from well-decorated mementos to be brought back from popular watering places and spas to the extravaganza of highly decorated and coloured glass of the late Victorian period. The catalogues of the nineteenth-century exhibitions show that there was a wide public demand for glass of all kinds, from vessels engraved with Greek motifs inspired by the Elgin marbles to vast coloured chandeliers fit for a maharajah's palace.

Much of this glass was produced in glasshouses or factories by unknown workers, though a few particularly gifted artists were known by name, but in the late

of etching and wheel-engraving. A stream of sand or crushed flint is directed onto the glass, and the pattern is achieved by protecting parts with a steel stencil plate or painted-on "resist".

The changing market

In early times glass was a luxury article, and tells us much about the people who used it. The small Egyptian and Syrian bottles made by the slow core-winding method were intended for perfume or as containers for oils used in elaborate burial rites, while the masterpieces of Roman cameo, "cage", mosaic and *millefiori* glass were the possessions of wealthy noblemen. Many of these ancient techniques were revived in Renaissance Venice, whose glassworkers also supplied a luxury-loving, rich clientele.

Eventually rebelling against the tight controls of the "Serenissima", some brave glass-workers took their skills over the Alps through France and into Holland. Here in the North were the two emerging maritime powers, the Dutch and the English, who were to make their fortunes through maritime adventures, build elegant houses lit by brilliant glass chandeliers and drink fine wines from

Below Enhancing the magnificent ball-room of the Assembly Rooms in Bath, designed by John Wood the Younger in 1771, are stunning chandeliers, five in all. During World War II the room was all but destroyed by enemy bombs, but luckily the chandeliers had been put into storage and were thus saved. The numerous swags of crystal festooning these three massive candle fixtures were a common element of Neoclassical chandeliers in England.

nineteenth and early twentieth centuries individual glass artists began to emerge – figures such as Gallé, Marinot and Lalique – who were fascinated by the properties of glass and produced pieces which are works of art in their own right. For glass has special qualities and endless potential as an art medium – the play of light both within it and from it, its brilliance when cut, the range of possible colours and its amazing plasticity. These attributes, combined with the skill and artistry of the glassmaker, can produce objects which are both useful and a source of wonder and delight.

Below Internal trailed decoration creates balloon-like forms on this contemporary glass bowl. It was made in 1977 by English glass artist Pauline Solven, who studied at the Royal College of Art with Sam Herman, an American who was instrumental in sparking the Studio Glass movement in Great Britain.

Above Before the fashion for suspending elaborate crystal chandeliers from ceilings became widespread in the eighteenth century, fairly simple standing table chandeliers were in use such as this lead-glass English example of c.1695. It has four candle-nozzles with drip-pans surmounting smooth, curving arms, and the central stem, foot and finial are likewise smooth, though nicely formed with vari-sized knops.

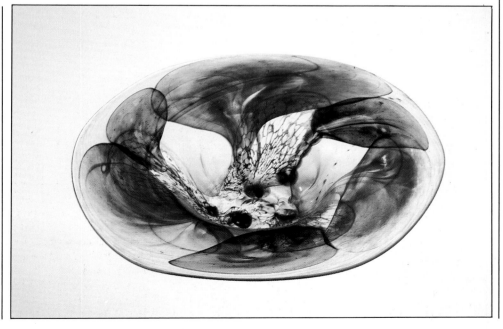

Ewer with wheel-cut decoration, late tenth century AD.

CHAPTER·ONE
EGYPT, ROME AND ISLAM

EGYPT, ROME AND ISLAM

Although glass was first made in Mesopotamia in Western Asia, the earliest datable glass objects come from Ancient Egypt. As early as 4000 BC stone beads were being covered with a glass glaze and coloured with a copper compound to imitate the costlier turquoise and lapis lazuli. The earliest glass vessels, however, are considerably later, of the New Kingdom or 18th Dynasty period (1567-1320 BC). They were made by the "sand core" method, which was used by the Egyptians for the amazingly long period of about 2000 years. The glass was melted in crucibles or pots and drawn out into threads which were wound around a sand and clay core held on an iron bar, which was used as a handle during the manufacture. The glass was repeatedly re-heated and softened threads of different colours were tooled or "combed" into zig-zag, festooned or feathered decorations.

Vessels produced by this method are necessarily small, and most of them were intended for toilet use, to contain unguents, fragrant oils and cosmetics. They were brilliantly coloured, displaying a high degree of excellence, and would have been costly and highly prized – not only for use during life but equally important to accompany the dead on the journey to eternal life in the next world. Amulets, to be worn during life or laid among the bandages of the mummy after death, were also made from glass, which was used as a substitute for precious stones.

The Egyptian court of the New Kingdom enjoyed unparalleled wealth and luxury, and glass manufactories seem to have been based at major urban centres and came under royal or aristocratic patronage. Pieces of glass bearing the names of kings of this period are known, for example there are three with the cartouche of Tuthmosis III; the grave of Amenhotep II (1448-1420 BC) contained glass vessels bearing his cartouche; and the Victoria and Albert Museum has the bezel of a ring with that of Queen Tiyi, wife of Amenhotep III. The great city of Tell-el Amarna (or Akhetaten), built by Akhenaten for his new religious cult, had a glass manufactory on the northern edge of the south residential quarter, which indicates the importance attached to glass. Quantities of broken glass were found in the nearby waste-heaps, some with simple engraved patterns.

Glass was also used in the form of mosaic inlay. Patterns were composed by assembling rods of coloured glass, drawing out the rod and then cutting pieces transversely, essentially a form of *millefiori* glass. The tomb of Tutankhamen contained an unusual headrest made from two large pieces of turquoise-coloured glass, and the king's golden throne was inlaid with coloured glass, faience and carnelian, with the faces and parts of the bodies of the king and queen in red glass inlay.

The period of 1220-1000 BC in Egypt was one of

Above This barrel-shaped scent bottle in colourless glass was made by blowing, with the bands at each end trailed on. It dates from the late second century AD, and came from Germany, probably Cologne. Similar examples are known in metal.

Right This greenish-colourless blown bottle with complex trailing is of a very rare type and is known as "the Masterpiece" of the small group to which it belongs. It was found in Cologne in 1893, and is thought to date from the second half of the third century AD. A bottle with similar trailing was found in Nijmegen in Holland, but it is thought that this style of decoration went out of fashion in Roman Cologne at the end of the third century AD.

decline, corruption and instability. The country was attacked from Africa in 1220 and again in 1189 and 1186. A "dark age" spread across the Eastern Mediterranean and Western Asia, disrupting commerce and manufacturing, and little glass has been found on archeological sites between 1200 and 1000 BC.

Western Asia
There was a glass industry in Mesopotamia contemporaneous with that in Egypt, the earliest datable objects being beads, seals and inlays. Vessels appeared towards the end of the sixteenth century BC, usually based on contemporary pottery forms. The manufacture of glass spread quickly after this to Syria, Cyprus and the Aegean, Anatolia and the Syro-Palestinian area; there must have been a flourishing glass industry in most civilized settlements of the Eastern Mediterranean. As in Egypt, glass was considered a rare and precious material for use in luxury items, on a par with metals, stones and ivory.

Around 1200 BC the leading centres came under attack and collapsed. The Mycenaean and Minoan civilizations totally vanished, as did the powerful Hittite kingdom in Anatolia, and Palestine was invaded by the Philistines. From the tenth century BC, however, new peoples rose to prominence in the Eastern Mediterranean: the Phrygians of Anatolia, the Assyrian empire of the Tigris-Euphrates valley area, the Greeks in the Aegean and the Phoenicians along the Palestinian seaboard. Due to the colonizing of the Greeks and the commercial ventures of the Phoenicians, Italy and the Western Mediterranean became part of the ancient world and its culture.

The glassmaking centres of Mesopotamia and then Syria also produced core-formed vessels – using the same techniques and colours as the earlier examples, but with different shapes. In the sixth century, core-formed bottles based on Greek pottery shapes, containers for scents and oils, were produced in the Syrian centres. Tablewares, made by casting and usually in green glass, and drinking bowls also appeared; many examples of the latter were excavated at Nimrud, the Assyrian capital. Small flasks which were cast and then cut, ground and polished, are known – one of these, also found at Nimrud, is now in the British Museum and known as the Sargon vase. These bear a strong resemblance to silver and bronze containers, as do the cast and cut bowls produced in Iran in the fifth and fourth centuries BC after the overthrow of the Assyrians by the Persians.

In the middle of the fourth century BC Macedonia became a major military power under Philip II and then his son Alexander the Great, who vanquished the Persians and founded his own empire which included most of the civilized world. After his death in 323 BC the empire was divided into separate Hellenistic kingdoms: Egypt under the Ptolemies, Syria and Mesopotamia under the Seleucid kings, and Macedon and Greece under the Antigonids. In the West the Etruscans were attacked by the Carthaginians and later by the Romans.

In the Hellenistic Empire glass tableware in the form of bowls was produced, in both clear and brilliantly coloured glass. These were made by casting in or over moulds and were then lathe- or wheel-ground to their final shape; some are fluted and some have lathe-cut rings. They have been found (and were probably made) in the north-east Mediterranean area, and again show strong affinities with contemporary metal examples.

At the same time the technique of sandwich gold glass, in which gilt decoration is trapped between two layers of clear glass, was perfected, and the mosaic technique revived, to produce brilliantly and multi-coloured vessels. In Greek settlements in Southern Italy efforts were made to create whole table services, with both serving and drinking vessels; these, which include plates, shallow dishes, footed bowls, hemispherical bowls and cups with and without handles, were made in clear, purple, deep blue and mosaic glass.

Other examples found are elegant *reticelli* (lace mosaic) bowls and vessels with cut panels of gold leaf between two blanks of clear glass. These, which date from the early to mid-second century BC, were luxury wares. Glass had been considered extremely precious at the beginning of the Hellenistic period, but by the end it was in more general use, and has been found on most Hellenistic sites and in large quantities.

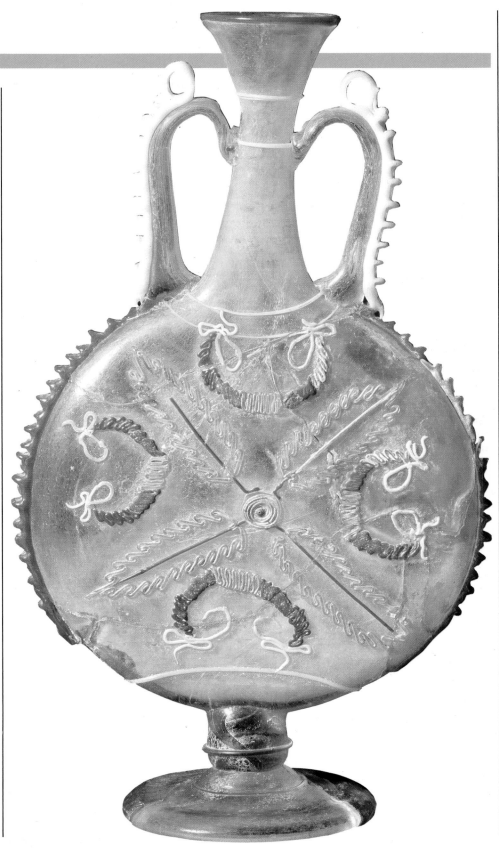

17

A rare drinking horn in light green glass dating from the fourth century AD and found in Cologne.

The Roman Empire

While Italy and the Western Mediterranean had become a part of the ancient civilized world due to the colonizing and commercial ventures of the Greeks, the Romans themselves now became the conquerors. By 201 BC they had vanquished the Western Mediterranean, and in 30 BC effectively ended the Hellenistic period when Augustus incorporated Egypt, which had been the last independent kingdom in the Eastern Mediterranean, into the Roman Empire, which thus comprised most of the known world.

Important glassworks were established in Rome and other parts of Roman Italy in the first century AD. They continued to use the casting method (some in two-part moulds) and show a great range of new shapes, colours and decoration. They include bowls in coloured glass (usually blue, purple or yellow), marbled mosaic and bluish-green and light green glass.

The discovery of glassblowing (most probably in the Syro-Palestinian area) revolutionized the glass industry, cutting down both costs and production time and allowing a much greater range of shapes and sizes. By the middle of the first century AD blown glass had supplanted cast wares, and according to Pliny the Elder, glassworks had spread to Gaul and Spain. Also during Pliny's time glass was used as wall tiles, especially in bathrooms, and glass mosaics were used as interior decoration – the finest and most detailed were found at Hadrian's villa at Tivoli.

From this time onwards there was a vast production of ordinary domestic glassware, but there was also a demand for luxury glass. The most spectacular decorated vessels of the Augustan period are the rare cameo glasses, cups,

This fine portrait bust of the Emperor Augustus (27 BC – AD 14) is made of dark blue glass and was probably cast in a mould using the lost wax or cire-perdue technique. The thick turquoise layer is the result of weathering, which has also caused some iridescence. Analysis has shown that this turquoise layer comes from copper and iron (found in considerable quantities). Lead, tin and manganese are also present, and it has been conjectured that the lead may have been inserted in a free-standing gold or silver statuette. Only a few miniature heads of Roman Emperors have survived in glass, and this one may have been made in Rome or Alexandria.

vases and amphorae like the famous Portland vase. Cameo glass was made by superimposing white opaque glass on a base of coloured glass (usually blue or purple). The layer of white was then cut away in places to reveal the ground colour, and the remaining white areas were carved by a gem cutter with relief scenes.

Equally breathtaking, and among the finest examples of the glassmakers' art ever produced, were the cage, or *diatreta*, cups. They were made during the fourth century, but their exact place of manufacture is not known. They

18

were produced by making a thick-walled blank of the required shape, either in colourless glass or with bands of several colours. This was then cut away to create an openwork pattern attached to the background wall with a minimum of bridges. The famous Lycurgus cup in the British Museum is the best-known example of this amazing technique. The carving, which illustrates the death of the Thracian king Lycurgus, is incredible enough, but the treatment of the colouring is also outstanding. Because of the presence of minute amounts of gold and silver, added to the mix of glass, the colour changes from green in reflected light to magenta in transmitted light.

Concurrent with these productions went a revival of the technique of sandwich gold glass in Rome, with Christian, Jewish and mythological scenes etched in gold leaf. Examples are rare, and almost all the known fragments have been found in Roman catacombs, where they were cemented into tombs. It was a technique which was to be exploited again many centuries later – in the Bohemian *zwischengoldglas* of the late eighteenth and early nineteenth centuries.

Byzantine and Islamic glass

With the collapse of the unity of the Roman Empire in the fourth and fifth centuries AD and the removal of the official capital to Constantinople in AD 330, there was a very definite division between East and West, with the technical standards and luxury market going to the East. Little is known of early Byzantine glass, although its rulers appear to have actively encouraged the art – the Emperor Constantine in 337 exempted glass-makers from all public levies. Syro-Palestinian workmen continued to make glass until the conquest in AD 632 by the armies of Islam. Their productions include small bottles and jugs probably used as containers of holy oil (*eulogia*) and sold to pilgrims in Jerusalem. Another type is a small bottle mounted on the back of a horse and enclosed in trailed latticework – generally ascribed to the sixth to the eighth centuries, and found from Jerusalem to the Euphrates.

A Byzantine provenance has been claimed for a series of vessels known as Hedwig glasses. They are decorated with high relief and intaglio cutting, and came to be associated with the miracle of St Hedwig (1174-1243), patron saint of Silesia. They are in smoky-brown or green-tinted glass cut with such motifs as lion, eagle, griffin, palm leaves and so on, and have been found from western Germany and Poland to Russia, though their true origin remains a mystery.

Before the Arab conquest of Mesopotamia and Persia (now Iraq and Iran) there had been a flourishing glass industry under the Sassanian emperors, which came to be profoundly influenced by the Arab invasions which spread through Egypt and North Africa to Persia and as

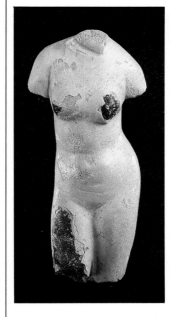

A model of a female torso, in pale yellowish-green glass, covered with a layer of flesh-coloured weathering. It was made by casting, and the details were wheel-cut. This would once have been a complete figure, and is a miniature version of the Aphrodite of Knidos, a life-size sculpture of the third century BC, which was much copied in the first and second centuries AD.

far west as Spain. By the eighth century the Arábs had achieved a political unification of Western Asia and the Southern Mediterranean under one ruler – the Abbasid dynasty (750-1258) – with Baghdad in Mesopotamia as its capital.

Here it was that a recognizably Islamic art was born. Glass excavated at Samarra, fifty miles north of Baghdad, where the Abbasid caliphs lived (833-83) shows facet, relief and linear cutting, and this bevelled style of cutting was also used by carvers and moulders on stucco and wood decoration.

The Muslim invasion of Spain produced a strong and long-lasting Moorish-Islamic influence on glassware and pottery, and lustre painting, first practised in Egypt in early Islamic times and in Persia in the ninth century, was introduced. Persia became a producer of fine glassware under the Samanid dynasty (AD 819-1004), with cut and engraved glass one of its major productions. The hard-stone engravers of Persia and Mesopotamia were probably the inspiration for another form of glass cutting in which the surface of the glass was ground down, leaving the decoration in relief on wafer-thin vessel walls. They also used the techniques of casting, stamping, pincer-work, lustre painting and applied work of the early Islamic period.

Glasses with coloured enamels and gilt inscriptions appear to have been produced in northern Syria c. 1170-1270. Among this group are beakers with motifs of animals, birds, human figures and arabesque foliage. The famous beaker known as the "Luck of Edenhall", probably brought back to the West by a traveller or Crusader, is of this period.

In the thirteenth century, Genghis Khan's armies conquered Mongolia, and then Persia, and sacked Baghdad in 1258. Syria was left to become the main glass-making centre of the Islamic Empire, and it was to reach its greatest achievements in the enamelled and gilt products of the thirteenth and fourteenth centuries, which became famous in the Near East. Both Aleppo and Damascus became centres – a European writer travelling in Syria in 1345-6 mentions "the street of the glass painters" in Damascus.

The great decorated mosque lamps were the most celebrated of Damascus wares. They were suspended in great numbers from the mosque ceilings by chains and lit the interior of many *madrasehs* (Muslim schools). They first appear about 1280, and carried on into the fourteenth century, when the decoration became less elaborate. Both they and related glass products ceased to be made in Damascus when history intervened once again in the shape of Timur, or Tamerlaine, who captured the city in 1400 and forcibly or otherwise removed the skilled workers to his capital of Samarkand.

INSPIRATIONS

The potter's craft was already well established when glass first made its appearance, and before its potential as a material in its own right was recognized, it was used as a glaze for ceramics. Later it was fashioned into beads as a substitute for the costlier semiprecious stones, and these were exported far and wide. Another use was as a form of mosaic inlay (**1**) together with stones and coloured ceramic pieces.

The brilliant blue seen on much Egyptian glass imitates the semiprecious stones turquoise and lapis-lazuli, as does this ceramic fritware (**2**) on which copper was used to produce the intense colour.

1

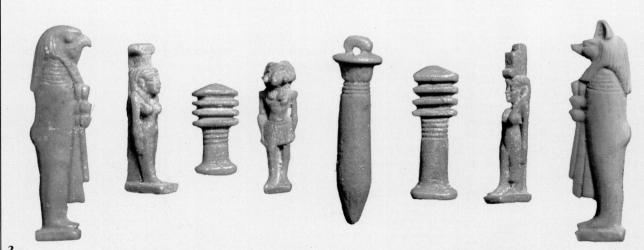

2

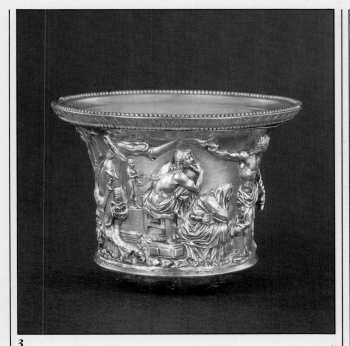

3

4

5

The discovery of glassblowing enabled a considerably greater output, and in Roman times the art of the glassmaker reached heights that were not to be equalled until Renaissance Venice. The intricate decoration and scenes from mythology that graced the silver vessels of the period (3,4) were also worked on the costlier items of luxury glass, such as the cage cups and cameo vases.

Mosaics such as this delightful first-century BC example (5) decorated the walls of most well-to-do citizens of the Roman Empire, and glass was also used for this purpose. Glass mosaics applied to niches, columns and fountains can be seen at Pompeii, and later were to impart a wonderful glow of colour to Byzantine churches.

ANCIENT EGYPT

1 *This lovely scent bottle in the shape of a fish comes from Tell-el-Amarna, the city founded by Akhenaten for his new but short-lived faith.*

2 *An Egyptian* amphoriskos *also for use as a perfume or oil bottle, in a deep blue glass with combed decoration in white and yellow. This small masterpiece is of the 18th Dynasty of the New Kingdom – that is c.1400-1360 BC. Glassblowing was only discovered at a much later date, and these vessels were made by the laborious "sand-core" method, which was in use for about 2000 years.*

1

2

3

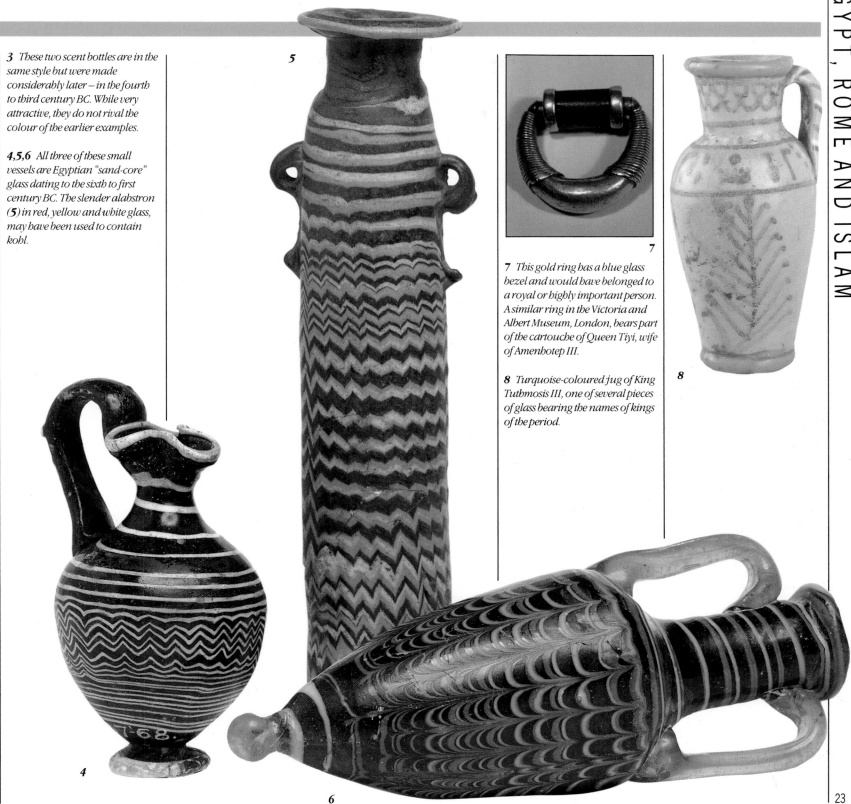

3 These two scent bottles are in the same style but were made considerably later – in the fourth to third century BC. While very attractive, they do not rival the colour of the earlier examples.

4,5,6 All three of these small vessels are Egyptian "sand-core" glass dating to the sixth to first century BC. The slender alabstron (**5**) in red, yellow and white glass, may have been used to contain kohl.

7 This gold ring has a blue glass bezel and would have belonged to a royal or highly important person. A similar ring in the Victoria and Albert Museum, London, bears part of the cartouche of Queen Tiyi, wife of Amenhotep III.

8 Turquoise-coloured jug of King Tuthmosis III, one of several pieces of glass bearing the names of kings of the period.

5

7

8

4

6

ROMAN CAST AND POLISHED

1 *This box and cover dating from the first century AD is extremely rare, if not unique, for its size and shape. It is of blue glass and is cast, lathe turned and polished. It was found near Rome, and is described in the museum list as containing ashes. However, it is not known if it was used as a cinerary urn – or indeed what the original purpose may have been.*

2 *Probably dating from the second half of the first century AD, this piece, made of translucent dark blue glass and cast, wheel cut and polished, has been attributed to the Eastern Mediterranean or Italy. It is presumably the cover of a fish-shaped dish. The cutting of the detail has been very carefully executed.*

1

2

3 The ribbed bowl in dark blue glass, dating from the third quarter of the first century, was made in the Roman Empire, probably in Italy, as many such bowls have been found there. They are a continuation of examples found in the Eastern Mediterranean during the first century BC, which have shorter ribs or widely spaced "knob" ribs. By the end of the century the ribs had become longer and more regular. Apsley Pellatt Jnr of the Falcon Glassworks gave them the name "pillar-moulded" bowls, and they have been popularly known thus ever since.

3

4 This elegant boat-shaped cast bowl made of translucent green glass dates from the second quarter of the first century AD, and was found at Pompeii, Italy. It is said to have held jewellery when found, and it is possible that such bowls were used on ladies' dressing tables, as a number have been found in female graves. The feet were added separately to the bowl, the joints being ground smooth. The shape can be identified with cargo vessels, which appear in relief carvings, frescoes and mosaics.

4

ROMAN CAMEO

1 *The Portland vase is probably the most famous piece of glass known, and is certainly the one with the most dramatic history. It is known to have been broken on three occasions, first at some time in antiquity when the disc now in the base was attached; this is not the original base, indeed some authorities believe that the vase could have been a pointed vessel. It was damaged again between 1786 and 1809 by the Duchess of Gordon, and in 1810 the Duke of Portland, then its owner, loaned it to the British Museum, where in 1845 it and its case were smashed by a young man visiting the museum.*

There have been many interpretations of the scenes on the vase – the birth of Alexander the Great being one suggestion and the story of Achilles another. No one can even agree as to whether the two sides of the vase represent the same story or two separate scenes.

The industry for making cameo glass vessels would seem to have been short-lived – perhaps only seventy-five years from about 25 BC to about AD 40-60. It is not certain exactly where it was centred, although the greatest market for glass would no doubt have been in Rome. Because of certain similarities between some of the known examples it is possible that they came from the same workshop, but what is beyond all doubt is that these pieces are masterpieces of glassmakers' and engravers' art.

1

2

4

2 It is not known for certain how this piece, known as the Morgan cup, was made, but it is likely that the bowl was cast in blue glass and then covered in white glass by trailing up to a level below the rim. It was then cut on a wheel and engraved to produce the white relief design and finished by turning on the lathe. Because the style of the engraving is different from that on the Portland vase, some believe it to be pre-Roman, but it is more generally thought to date to the first half of the first century AD. It was formerly in the collection of J. Pierpont Morgan, hence its name.

3 This small fragment of a cameo glass bowl is carved in white relief against a blue background with a nude figure of a warrior, his cloak over his left arm. It dates to the early first century AD.

3

4 The Auldjo jug was formed by taking a "gather" of blue glass, partly casing it in white glass and then blowing. The upper part of the "paraison", or glass bubble, was then cut, leaving a strip to form the handle. The body is cameo-engraved with a design of birds, flowering scrolls and vines entwined with laurel and ivy leaves. The jug dates to the second or third quarter of the first century AD, and was found at Pompeii between 1830 and 1832.

27

ROMAN OPENWORK

1

2

1 Cage-cups, or vasa diatreta, were the most expensive and highly prized kind of glass in Roman times, and the glass-cutters (diatretarii) enjoyed special privileges, such as being exempt from tax on their homes and workplaces. This rare example has three-colour overlay. The bowl was cast in colourless glass, the red and yellow trailed on and the green on the lower part cased on. The decoration was then cut away and supported only by bridges attaching it to the body. It was excavated from a grave in a family cemetery at Cologne, but it is not certain where the cage-cups were made, as some have also been found in the Near East.

2 This two-handled cup on stem, said to have been found in Cologne in 1864, is not a vasa diatreta, as the bowl is blown and the cagework and handles are trailed on. The outside of the cup (under the cagework) is decorated with gold foil engraved with three cupids amidst flowers. The upper part of the goblet is missing – it would have risen at least another 5cm/2in, probably cylindrically. After a chemical analysis of the glass it has now been dated to the late third or early fourth century AD.

3 Another rare cage cup dating from c. 300 AD, in colourless glass with opaque honey-coloured weathering. It is of hemispherical shape with a rounded base, either blown or cast, and cut with three concentric rings of "mesh". It is said to have been found in Syria.

4 The famous Lycurgus cage-cup, dating from the fourth century AD, was probably mould-blown. One of its most remarkable features is that the opaque green glass turns to red in transmitted light because of the presence of colloidal gold and silver in the glass. The thick-walled blank was cut and ground, leaving large portions of the frieze design standing almost free, connected only by bridges. The decoration depicts the death of Lycurgus, King of the Thracians, who fell foul of Dionysus and the Maenads, one of whom changed into a vine shoot, and wound herself around his neck. It has been suggested that this, like other Dionysiac vessels in both glass and silver, was for ritual use in pagan circles.

5 The tall goblet, found in a cremation grave in Cologne and dating from the early fourth century AD, is blown in greenish glass and has applied trails of flowers enclosed in panels by a network of eight vertical straps. Four of these have mussel shell motifs, which seem only to occur in Cologne. The bottle is made in the same way but without the trailed decoration. It was also found in Cologne, and appears to date from the third century AD.

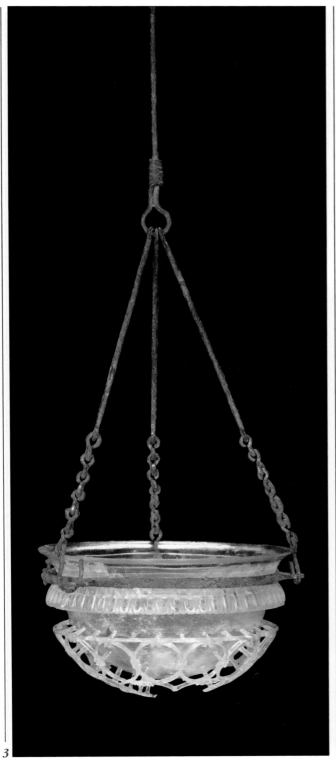

3

4

5

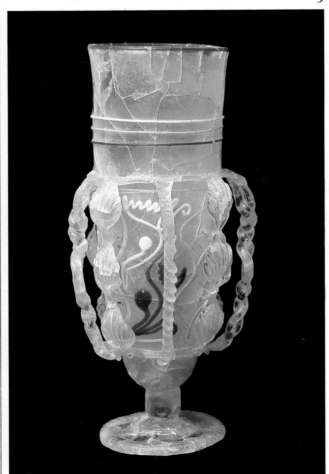

ROMAN UNDECORATED

1 *Cinerary urn, late first to second century AD. Made of bluish glass, and blown, the vessel has an attached strap handle with nineteen ribs at the base. Although bottles of this kind were certainly used as cinerary urns when cremation was commonly practised, they were probably more often made as receptacles for storage of wine and other liquids. Large quantities of undecorated Roman blown glass have survived and have been found all over the area encompassed by the Roman Empire. This example comes from Flamersheim in Germany.*

1

2

3

2 This bird-shaped bottle, of the first century AD, is of a type fairly common in North Italian and Alpine regions, although it is not known where this example was found. It is blown in light blue glass and has patches of silvery weathering and some iridescence. The vessels may have contained perfume or some type of cosmetic; the bottle was heat-sealed after filling, and would have been opened by breaking the top of the bird's tail.

3 This large bowl, in light yellow glass with deep purple spiral streaks, is blown in a slightly distorted oval shape. The foot was added by the so-called "poet technique", which involves taking a portion of molten glass from a cylinder formed on a second "paraison", or glass bubble. The type and colouring is typical of fourth- to fifth-century Egyptian tableware from Kevanis, in the Faiyum (or Delta), although oval dishes were rare elsewhere.

ROMAN CUT AND ENGRAVED

1 A blown jug in clear glass, decorated all over with fourteen rows of hexagonal wheel-cut facets (except under the applied handle). The ridge below the rim may have been the seating for a stopper. This shape is also known in pottery, for example there is an African red-slip jug in the British Museum dating from the first century AD, but in the style of cutting and polishing such vessels are a progression from the styles of a hundred years earlier.

2 A blown bowl in green-tinted colourless glass point-engraved with a scene of Eve about to take an apple from the tree in the Garden of Eden. The inscription translates as "Rejoice in God, Drink and may you live". The bowl was found in a grave in the Luxemburger Strasse, Cologne, in 1902–3 and came from a glass workshop in Cologne which was working from the third decade of the fourth century AD.

3 This blown pale green glass bottle, known as the Populonia bottle, belongs to a group of nine vessels, all of similar shape, bearing wheel-abraded decoration showing waterfront scenes and inscriptions. The scenes include a lake, a palace, a harbour wall with four arches on the columns and a double-arched building topped by four horses. This example was found in a grave at ancient Populonia in Tuscany.

MOSAIC AND MILLEFIORI

1 *The rosette-like canes in these bowls are sometimes called millefiori – a thousand flowers. This is not an ancient term, but was coined when the technique was revived in Venice in Renaissance times. In the nineteenth century the same method was much used for French paperweights.*

2 *This beautiful bowl with its blue and yellow twist rim is made up of fifty-seven pre-formed lace-mosaic canes laid side by side and "sagged" in a mould. Both interior and exterior are polished. Present evidence indicates that such bowls may have been made in Italy.*

2

1

3

3 *The shallow shape of this bowl is similar to a group dating from the early first century BC, although the style of canes is inspired by earlier Hellenistic mosaic work of the second and third centuries BC. The canes are fused in a mould, and both the interior and exterior are finely polished.*

4 *A fragment of a mosaic panel used to decorate a wall. This form of decoration must have been used extensively in prosperous homes and public buildings, especially during the first century AD. Remains found at Herculaneum show panels mostly made up of small coloured-glass cubes.*

4

5

5,7 *These magnificent examples, made by arranging fragments of coloured glass side by side and then fusing them together, were possibly an attempt to imitate the stone, sardonyx. "Murrhine" bowls, which may have been made of patterned semi-precious stones, were famous in ancient times, mentioned by Pliny among others.*

6 *This bowl is also ground and polished, but is especially interesting for the four square canes bearing a female head-and-shoulders portrait, in which the woman is shown wearing a coral type necklace. A bead in the Corning Glass Museum has a similar design.*

6

7

1

1 *Blown in green-tinted colourless glass, this bowl is painted with a duck heading towards a net which is, presumably, a snare. It dates from the first century AD, and is thought to have been made in northern Italy in a workshop founded by Syrian workers, as typical Syrian styles have been used. It has been suggested that the famous Ennion (see page 38) might have had a workshop in Italy.*

2 *The Daphne ewer, dating from the late second to early third century AD, is blown in translucent and opaque white glass, and has a ribbed handle attached to the shoulder and rim. It was found in a tomb at Kerch in the Crimea and it is thought that it may have been made at a workshop in Antioch-on-the-Orontes. It is painted in red, grey and gilding with the story of Daphne, which gives it its name, and has an inscription in Greek capitals. Daphne (laurel) was loved and pursued by the god Apollo, but when she spurned his advances and prayed for help, the gods turned her into a laurel tree.*

3 *This portrait medallion, dating from the late second to early third century AD, was made by casting a blue glass disc, applying gold leaf and drawing the decoration with a fine point in the gold. An upper disc of clear glass was then fused over the top. It was probably intended as an object in its own right and not one to be included as decoration on a vessel; such medallions are known as decorations to graves in the catacombs.*

4 *This small bottle, dating from the third to fourth century AD, is blown in a green-tinted colourless glass, painted in white, yellow, red, blue and black, and gilded. It also has Greek inscriptions. It is possible that this, like the Daphne ewer, was made in Syria. It tells the story of Marsyas and Apollo. The goddess Athena invented the flute but threw it away when she discovered it distorted the features of the player. Marsyas rescued the flute and became so skilful in playing it that he challenged Apollo to a contest with his lyre. The Muses gave the victory to Apollo, but the god was so angry at the presumption of Marsyas that he had him tied to a tree and flayed alive.*

2

3

4

SYRIAN GLASSMAKERS

1

2

3

1 This two-handled drinking cup is mould-blown and bears the legend "Ennion made it" in Greek. On the reverse is another inscription "Let the buyer remember", also in Greek. From the places in which glass with the name of this famous maker has been found, it seems likely that he (and other glassmakers) worked at Sidon on the Syrian coast. Mould-blowing was probably a direct development of casting in a mould which was in widespread use in the Syro-Palestinian region in later Hellenistic times. It is not possible to date Ennion's activities precisely, but on present evidence it would seem that he was active in the early decades of the first century AD.

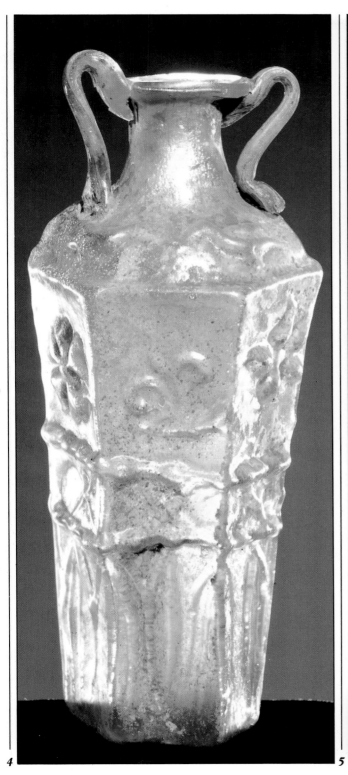

2 *Ennion has also been suggested as the maker of these lidded boxes (pyxides). The workmanship is of high quality, with the lids fitting the bases extremely well. This example is of yellowish-brown glass, blown in a three-part mould, and with a garland of ivy leaves, buds and berries.*

3 *Another vessel made by Ennion, possibly to hold palm oil, and also marked in Greek "Ennion made it". It is of yellowish-brown glass, blown in a four-part mould, and decorated with a border of palmette motifs on the shoulders above a wide band of honeycomb pattern and a lower band of gadroons. The elegant handle is applied.*

4 *This very rare scent bottle in greenish glass with surface iridescence is similar to a hexagonal one signed "Ennion", which was found in Cyprus. This example, decorated with five-leaf stars and leaf motifs and blown in a two-part mould, has very unusual applied handles.*

5 *This colourless glass head-flask, with its finely modelled features and hair, is very rare in having the inscription "Eugenes", probably the name of the glassmaker, below the chin. At the back it has another inscription "May you prosper Melanthus". It was found in a tomb near ancient Idalium in Cyprus, and dates from the first century AD.*

4

5

SYRIAN GLASSMAKERS

1 *This large, elegant jug made in pale green glass was found in Syria and dates from the fourth century AD. It is blown, but not in a mould, and has an applied handle with an upright thumbpiece. Similarly shaped jugs were also made in silver.*

2 *Another elegant jug similar in shape to (**1**) and with the same type of handle and thumbpiece, probably from Syria or Palestine. The vessel is decorated with three trails nipped together in a diamond pattern, while the neck has thick trails nicked to simulate a corded collar.*

1

2

3 *This "snake thread" dropper flask is certainly of Eastern origin. For many years it was thought that all such decorated wares originated in the Rhineland, but now it is believed that they originated in the East in the second century AD and were taken to the Cologne factories by migrant glass-workers during the same period. This example is of yellowish glass, blown and with applied and flattened snake trails with notched bodies. The surface has been weathered and shows iridescence.*

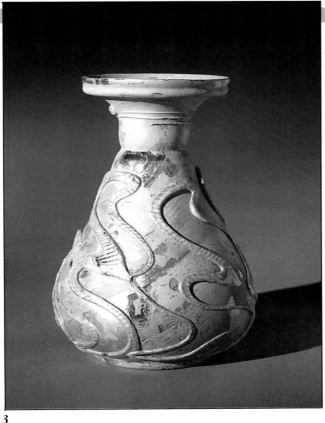

4 *A large and highly elaborate "basket-type" cage surmounting a four-compartment unguent bottle, dating to the beginning of the fifth century AD and definitely of Eastern type. Although unguent bottles are not uncommon, the intricacy of the cagework is very unusual. Made of green glass with a bluish-green handle, the piece was blown and the sides pinched in to form the compartments.*

5 *A selection of six mould-blown small flasks dating from the first to fourth centuries AD. From left to right: A Janus-head flask in greenish yellow glass, c. second century AD. A yellow amphoriskos moulded with vine tendrils, applied pale blue and violet-streaked handles, first to second century AD. A manganese-purple amphoriskos moulded with horizontal ribbing, first century AD. A manganese-purple sprinkler flask moulded with vertical ribbing, third to fourth century AD. An amber-coloured flask moulded as a date, with naturalistic wrinkled exterior, third to fourth century AD. A dark brown date flask, also naturalistically moulded, third to fourth century AD. These small vessels, which held perfumes and cosmetic oils, were popular over a long period of time, and many have been found in graves.*

3

4

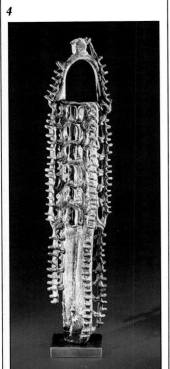

5

EARLY ISLAMIC

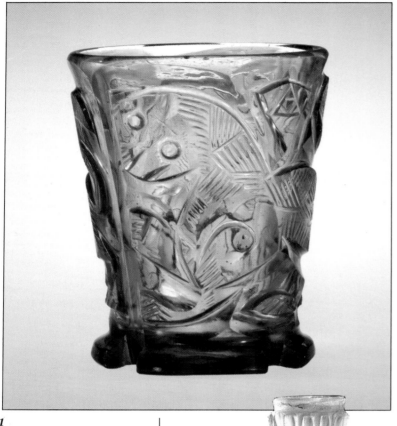

1 Literary sources of the Middle Ages record that engraved glass and rock crystal were considered as valuable as gold and silver. Many rock crystal and glass vessels found their way into the treasuries of European cathedrals, were used as reliquaries, and became associated with Christian beliefs. This beaker, which is blown in colourless glass and wheel-cut in high relief, is one of a series of vessels known as "Hedwig glasses" as they are similar to one believed to have belonged to St Hedwig, who died in 1243. It is thought to be Egyptian work of the twelfth century A.D.

2 The Islamic style is typified by a subordination of the individual motif into an intricate decorative effect. The flowing line of the engraving on the lower part of the body of this mould-blown bottle, dating from the second half of the ninth century AD, is close to the rock-crystal carving of Sassanian Persia. It is said to have been found in Nishapur.

3 The skilled craftsmanship of the lapidary, or stone cutter, is demonstrated by this rock-crystal ewer dating from the ninth to tenth centuries. Glass vessels of the same shape are known with decoration imitating the carved patterns. In Persia this art was brought to a high technical level, and Iraq also had a flourishing glassmaking centre at Samarra.

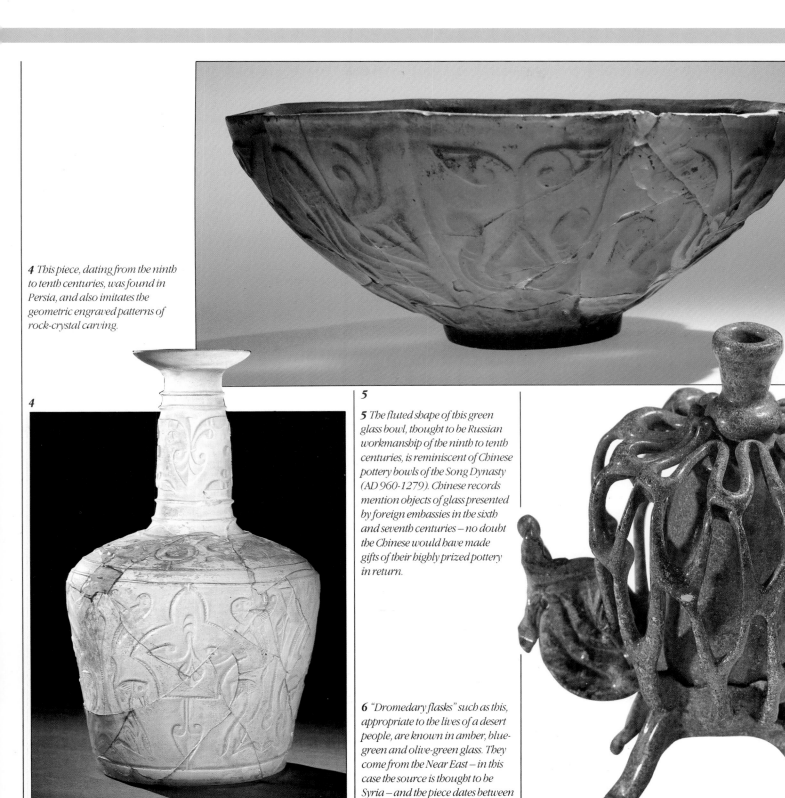

4 *This piece, dating from the ninth to tenth centuries, was found in Persia, and also imitates the geometric engraved patterns of rock-crystal carving.*

4

5

5 *The fluted shape of this green glass bowl, thought to be Russian workmanship of the ninth to tenth centuries, is reminiscent of Chinese pottery bowls of the Song Dynasty (AD 960-1279). Chinese records mention objects of glass presented by foreign embassies in the sixth and seventh centuries – no doubt the Chinese would have made gifts of their highly prized pottery in return.*

6 *"Dromedary flasks" such as this, appropriate to the lives of a desert people, are known in amber, blue-green and olive-green glass. They come from the Near East – in this case the source is thought to be Syria – and the piece dates between the sixth and eighth centuries.*

6

ISLAMIC ENAMELLING

1

2

3

4

4 *Chinese influence can be seen in this vase, dating from c. 1320-1330. It was probably enamelled at Damascus, where Chinese-inspired motifs appeared before the end of the thirteenth century; by this time the Mongols had overrun Asia and founded the Yuan Dynasty in China (1280). This influence is seen in a new naturalism and such motifs as lotus, peonies and cloud scrolls. The inscription on the vase repeats the Arabic word for "the Wise" – referring to Mohammed.*

5 *This famous cup or beaker is known as the Luck of Edenhall because it was a family heirloom of the Musgrave family of Edenhall. It is accompanied by an English cut-leather case dating from the end of the fourteenth century and was probably brought from Palestine by a Crusader. There are other examples in European collections, demonstrating the contacts with Syrian glassmakers during the Crusades.*

5

1 *Enamelled glass dates from the thirteenth century, and much of the finest work was done in Syria, where this bottle probably comes from. It dates from c. 1270, at which time enamelling was dominated by blue and red combined with opaque white and gold. The arms are believed to be of the Mameluke Sultan Baybars I (reigned 1260-1277).*

2,3 *The Egyptian mosque lamps are the best known of all the Islamic enamelled glass. The example (3) is an early one, and bears the name Sultan Baybars II, who was ruler of Egypt for only a few months before being executed in 1310. The other (2) is a little later, dating from about 1355. The motif of a cup in the panel on the rim records the office of "Cup-Bearer to the Sultan" to which a slave from the corps of pages could be promoted. In Mameluke Egypt a slave might be rapidly promoted to a high position, but was equally likely to fall rapidly to ruin.*

Bowl and cover in vetro a reticello, *early eighteenth century.*

CHAPTER·TWO
THE VENETIAN SUPREMACY

THE VENETIAN SUPREMACY

By the medieval period, Venice had become an important glassmaking centre, and by the Renaissance her supremacy in this field was unchallenged. To a large extent, her pre-eminence was an accident of geography. Not only was the city almost impregnable, with attack from sea or land virtually impossible, it was also perfectly placed to establish a complex network of trade links with Western Europe, Byzantium and the East. To support, widen and protect trade, the Republic of Venice had built a powerful mercantile fleet, whose ships were vitally necessary, among other things, for carrying the raw materials for the glasshouses.

The importance of the glass industry was quickly recognized, and the Senate of the Republic protected it with a number of laws and privileges. In 1268 the glassmakers were sufficiently established to take part, with other guilds, in the procession for the inauguration of the new doge, at which they carried "water bottles and scent flasks and other such graceful objects of glass".

In 1292 the Grand Council decreed the removal of all

Above *This dish in greyish-tinged* cristallo *glass was made c.1513-34 and bears the arms of a Medici pope, Leo X or Clement VII.*

Left *A fifteenth-century Venetian armorial cup and cover of elegant proportions, with wonderful swirling gilt ribs taking the eye upwards from the base to the top of the cover.*

Venetian glasshouses to the island of Murano, partly because of the risk of fire, but also to give a greater measure of control. But it also gave the industry the advantage of working in peaceful and isolated surroundings where they could, and did, put down roots and create strong traditions.

Venetian glass

In 1490 the Guild of Glassmakers was put under the direct jurisdiction of the Council of Ten, the highest body in the Venetian Republic. And in the next fifty years measures were taken which gave a high standard of living to the Muranese glassmakers but also imposed reprisals against any who left to set up a glasshouse elsewhere or divulged the secrets.

Glass was no longer a humble, utilitarian craft, but a highly valued, sophisticated art form, and before the end of the fifteenth century great glass masterpieces were being produced – armorial cups and covers and betrothal and marriage goblets – in brilliant shades of blue, turquoise and green richly enamelled and gilded. The products of Venice's glasshouses were highly prized by the great princes of Europe, and some special commissions have survived. One, in Breslau, is a magnificent cup with the arms of Hungary on one side and Bohemia on the other, almost certainly made for King Matthias Corvinus (d 1490), while in Budapest, from the site of the royal palace, fragments were recovered with the arms of Matthias' Queen, Beatrix of Aragon. The Museo Civico in Bologna has a pair of enamelled pilgrim flasks probably made for the marriage in 1492 of Alessandro Bentivoglio and Ippolita Sforza, and several glasses with the arms of Louis XII of France and Anne of Brittany, which may have been made for their marriage in 1499, have also survived.

Contemporaneous with the enamelled and coloured glasses were those made in opaque white glass – called

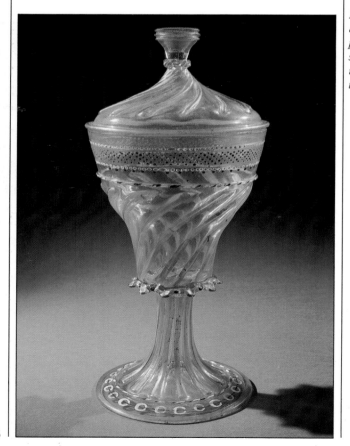

lattimo from the Italian word for milk, *latte*. These seem to have been made for the short span between 1475 and 1525. The opaque effect was achieved by adding oxide-of-tin to the mix, which was also used to glaze the wonderfully decorated *maiolica* ware of the time. But *lattimo* glass was essentially copying Chinese porcelain, interest in which had been kindled earlier by the great Venetian traveller Marco Polo, who returned from China in 1295. It had now become much valued; in 1561 the Doge Malipiero received a gift of it from the Sultan of Egypt.

The Venetian glassmakers' invention of *cristallo* glass was perhaps the result of looking for a substitute for rock crystal. Certainly its pureness and thinness fascinated people and created an overwhelming demand. It was produced by adding lime to the soda-silicate mixture, and although it is not known who invented it, it is now thought that Angelo Barovier (d 1460) of the famous Muranese glassmaking family may have played an important part. But whoever the glassmakers were, they blew and manipulated this featherweight material into the most elegant and fantastic shapes. They also sometimes trailed on blue glass to emphasize the outline of their ethereal forms.

At the same time they were producing remarkable designs by embedding opaque white canes in the glass, a technique called *vetro a filigrana* (known as *latticinio* in the nineteenth century). Although in 1527 two brothers, Filippo and Bernardo Serena, applied for a patent to make "glass of stripes with twists of cane", we know little of the makers of these wonderful glasses. When the canes of spiral and twisted coloured glass were used to make the *vetri a serpenti* they produced wonders of delightful extravagance – and extravagant in both senses of the word, for one of these glasses cost five times as much as an ordinary wine glass.

The complete antithesis of *cristallo* was ice glass, which was made in great quantities for export – Philip II of Spain so admired it that he owned sixty-five pieces. It was made by plunging a "gather" of glass into cold water for a moment and then blowing it, which enlarged the web of tiny cracks to give a sparkling, frosted appearance.

The Venetians also revived the Roman technique of *millefiori* glass towards the end of the fifteenth century. The colours at this time seem to have been opaque red, white and bright blue. However, such vessels are rare and were perhaps made as collectors' curiosities. Another rarity is chalcedony glass or *calcedonio*, made to imitate the precious and semi-precious stones collected by all the princely courts of Renaissance Europe. This gem mania reached its peak in the seventeenth century, and the glassworks were not to be outdone: Marcantonio Coccio Sabellico records that "there is no kind of precious stone

which cannot be imitated by the industry of the glass-workers, a sweet contest of nature and of man".

Diamond point engraving was used as decoration from the mid-sixteenth century, and was inspired by that used on metalwork. In 1549 Vicenzo di Angelo dall Gall is recorded as being given a licence to practise this technique, for which the soda-lime glass of Venice was eminently suitable. Quantities of *vetri intagliate* are listed in Murano in 1569 and 1577, so there must have been other workers capable of the skill.

Façon de Venise

It was inevitable that such a success story as the Muranese glass industry would be copied. There was such a demand for luxury glass throughout Renaissance Europe that multitudes of glasshouses began to spring up, all making glass in the Venetian style, so that it is often difficult to differentiate between that of Venice and that of other countries where Venetian-trained glass-blowers were in charge.

In Hall in Tirol a glassworks was founded in 1534 by Wolfgang Vitl of Augsburg, with Muranese and Altarist glassmakers (Altare in Italy had an established factory by 1282). In Bohemia, where glassmaking had been carried on since medieval times, there were twenty-four glass-houses by the sixteenth century. Professional glassmaking families, like the Preusslers and Schurers, started new houses in the Iserbirge and Riesengebirge regions, and although their glass was mainly of the Germanic type, with enamelled decoration, by the 1560s they also produced

Above Venetian glass was justly famed for its beauty, and glassworks sprang up all over Europe making wares in the same stlye, often supervised by Muranese workers. The scroll-stemmed façon de Venise goblet in the centre was made in Germany and the two tall flute glasses in the Netherlands – these were a Dutch speciality. The other glasses are mainly engraved in styles and techniqes developed at a later date in Germany and Bohemia.

filigree glass said to rival that of Venice and reputedly cheaper. They eventually made a potash glass which was stronger than the Venetian *cristallo*, and was capable of being wheel engraved (see Chapter Three). Bohemian glassmaking families moved around Germany, setting up glasshouses in Franconia and Thuringia, in Saxony and Brandenburg.

In Spain there was also much interest in Venetian glass, and there was a glasshouse in Barcelona whose products were said to rival those of Murano. But it was probably in the Low Countries (then Holland, Belgium and Northern France) that the largest quantity of *façon de Venise* glass was made. Antwerp, which was the largest seaport on the Atlantic seaboard, had strong trading links with Venice, and in 1558 a Muranese worker called Pasquetti started a glasshouse there which was to continue into the seventeenth century. Altarist glassmakers had also settled in

Left *German drinking glasses were made in several distinct types, some of which were based on medieval forms and continued with modifications throughout the sixteenth and seventeenth centuries. One such is the* passglas, *which could be plain, with ribbed divisions, engraved, as here, or enamelled.*

France, and established themselves in Paris, Nantes, Rouen and Bordeaux.

A contemporary catalogue of drawings illustrates the wide range of glasswares produced in these areas. Not only were simple *façon de Venise* bottles, flasks, wine cups and goblets made, but also elaborate luxury items like *nefs* (a galley-shaped wine vessel also made in silver and gold) and centrepieces. There are also illustrations of the decorative lion mask which was to become such a widespread and popular form of decoration on mould-blown stems.

In England luxury *façon de Venise* glassmaking arrived via the Netherlands. Up to the middle of the sixteenth century most glassmaking was confined to the Weald of Surrey and Sussex. But in 1567 Jean Carré, who had been connected with the glassmaking trade, arrived from Antwerp, and applied for and was granted two licences. One was to make "forest glass" (green or amber-tinted glass also known as *waldglas*) at Alford in the Weald and the second was to make glass "a la façon de Venise" at Crutched Friars in London, where he employed mainly Flemish workers.

After 1550, due to the persecution of the Protestants by the Catholics, large numbers of Huguenot refugees came to England to shelter under the sympathetic religious policy of Elizabeth I. In 1570 Carré brought over some Italians from Antwerp, one of whom was a Venetian, Jacopo Verzelini. He was master of the Crutched Friars glasshouse in 1572, and two years later, when Carré died, he obtained a patent for twenty-one years to make glass "in the Venetian manner"; the patent also forbade the import of Venetian glass from abroad. In 1592 Verzelini retired, leaving the glasshouse to be run by his sons.

German and Bohemian glass

Due to the rise of Protestantism and a flourishing merchant class in the Low Countries on the one hand and the decline of the Papacy and Italy on the other, the influence of Venice in glassmaking waned in the seventeenth century. The important centres moved from the South to the North of Europe, where the techniques of enamelling and diamond point engraving were to be developed and take on different national styles.

The elegant Venetian goblets and cups had been made for wealthy, aristocratic clients whose main drink was wine, but Northern Europe was catering for a rich merchant class. Their main drink was beer, drunk in larger quantities and from plainer glasses. One type made to meet this need was the *roemer* – a large bowl on a hollow prunted stem, and another was the *humpen* – a tall cylinder with "kick in" base, sometimes decorated with trailed and pincered bands, as on the *passglas*, which was passed around the company, each drinker being they were made in the glasshouses of the Holy Roman Empire throughout the seventeenth century and through Franconia, Fichtelgebirge and across Thuringia into Saxony, Silesia and Bohemia.

These glasses, like the humbler ones such as the *krautstrunk*, were given particular names according to the style of decoration. The *reichsadlerhumpen* bore the imperial eagle and symbols of the Empire, while *kurfurstenhumpen* (or Electors beakers) show the Emperor with the seven Electors of the Empire – originally from a sixteenth-century print by the Augsburg engraver Hans Vogel. The Fichtelgebirge area has a pine-clad mountain called the Ochsenkopf, and this appears on beakers called *Ochsenkopfhumpen*.

Humpen were also made for guilds, showing the members practising their craft; some were made for families, depicting and naming all the members of the family, and yet others had religious subjects from both Old and New Testaments. The *hofkellerenhumpen* (court cellar glass), which came from Saxony, had the arms and initials of the Elector of Saxony, and there were also bottles for use in the court pharmacy, many bearing the royal arms.

Up to this point we have little or no knowledge of individual glassmakers, but in the middle of the seventeenth century a new kind of glass-decorator appears in Germany – the *hausmaler*, who worked independently in his own small workshop, decorating both glass and faience (earthenware), which he obtained from the manufacturers undecorated.

These artists often signed and dated their work, and the first known was Johann Schaper from Nuremberg, originally a painter of stained window glass. He painted on both faience and glass, mostly in black (*schwarzlot*) with slight touches of red and gold, a completely different technique from the opaque enamelling on the *humpen*. Among Schaper's followers was Johann Ludwig Faber, also a window-glass and faience painter. These artists often used a small cylindrical beaker, sometimes on three bun feet, which is a typical Nuremberg shape.

Another exponent of *schwarzlot* decoration was the Nuremberger Abraham Helmhack (1654-1724), who also used a purple monochrome, and two slightly later artists were Daniel Preissler (1636-1733) and his son Ignaz (b 1670) working in Silesia and in Bohemia. Although they used the same colours, their style is very different from that of the Nuremberg workers. Their earlier work shows scenes of peasant life and hunting, while later they painted the popular chinoiserie figures and form of scroll and strapwork decoration known as *laub-und-bandelwerk*. Ignaz Preissler also painted on Chinese porcelain, and after about 1715 he is known as painting on Meissen porcelain.

Above *The humpen was a taller and wider version of the passglas, also made in both plain and decorated versions. The examples at left and right are Saxon armorial* humpen, *while the larger one in the centre has a painting in enamels representing the conversion of St Eustace. Enamelling was a popular form of decoration in Germany and Bohemia from the sixteenth century, and remained so for some time after it went out of fashion in Italy.*

apportioned his share by the divisions formed by the decoration.

Other popular drinking vessels were those made from "forest" or *wald* glass, and known as *krautstrunk* because their prunted decoration resembled rows of cabbage stalks and *warzenbecher* (wart or nipple beakers). The *kuttrolf*, which had between three and five tubes grouped round a narrow waist between body and neck, was of medieval origin, but was especially popular in the sixteenth and seventeenth centuries. Beaker-shaped glasses with embossments can also be traced through medieval types, right back to Roman origins. A somewhat childish (not to say barbaric) taste is seen in some puzzle glasses, used for practical jokes in drinking parties. In the Victoria and Albert Museum, London, there is a glass with a stag in the centre – the drinker had to suck the drink through the mouth of the stag.

The Venetian art of enamelling and gilding on glass was extremely popular in Germany and Bohemia, and indeed continued to be so after it had gone out of fashion in Italy. The glassmakers in Germany and Bohemia learned the secrets, and by the last quarter of the sixteenth century created a style of enamelling of their own which lasted for 150 years.

Humpen with enamelled decoration were first made in the sixteenth century. The Venetian glasshouses had first supplied rich German clients with this type of glass, but

INSPIRATIONS

Chinese porcelain (*1*) was highly prized in Renaissance Europe, and much Venetian glass, notably the opaque white glass called lattimo, attempted to imitate its qualities. The ingenious glassmakers of Murano also experimented with glass resembling semi-precious stones, as the Romans had done centuries earlier, and revived several of the Roman techniques, such as millefiori and sandwich glass (painted decoration enclosed between two layers of clear glass.

These two plates (*2*) in lattimo glass are painted in iron-red monochrome with highly realistic views of Venice inspired by etchings by Luca Carlevario. The glass enamellers and painters drew on both contemporary and antique sources for their subject matter and styles.

3

In the eighteenth century the secret of true porcelain was discovered at Meissen, and the Murano glassmakers rose to the challenge (*3*). Both the milky white glass and the enamelled floral decoration convincingly imitate the famed products of the German factory.

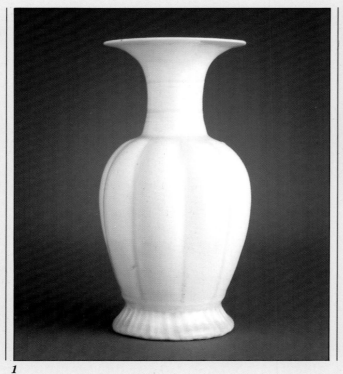

1

2

4

5

6

Gold or silver nefs, salt-cellars in the form of ships (**4**), were a popular ornament for the tables of the wealthy, and as the Venetian glassmakers became more and more skilled it was natural that they should also turn their hands to this kind of work (**5**). Venetian glass was far from being the poor relation of metalwork: the best of it was extremely expensive.

The so-called Aldrovandin beaker (**6**) is something of a mystery. Some experts claim that it is Syrian work, imported into Venice, while others believe it to be Venetian, dating from the fourteenth century, which seems more likely as it bears a Latin inscription. But whatever its provenance it is a testimony to the influence of Islamic enamelled glass on that of Venice. Because of the city's trade links with the Eastern Mediterranean, the Venetian glassworkers were certainly familiar with these artefacts, and mosque lamps were made in Venice for over a century – in 1569 the Venetian ambassador to Constantinople, then capital of the Ottoman Turks, mentions an order for 900 for a new mosque.

VENETIAN ARMORIAL

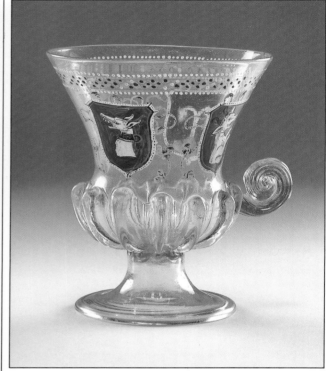

1 A covered cup in clear glass with elaborate surface decoration of white and coloured enamels and gilding in a scale pattern. The lid bears the date 1518 and two coats-of-arms.

2 A colourless glass armorial cup supported on a trumpet foot, dating from the early sixteenth century, a rare type which combines the Venetian goblet form with that of the Northern European handled cup. The band of scale pattern below the rim is gilt and enamel.

3 The Triumph of Venus cup, made in sapphire-blue glass, dates from the mid-fifteenth century. The quality of the drawing and the enamelling are less sophisticated than on later examples.

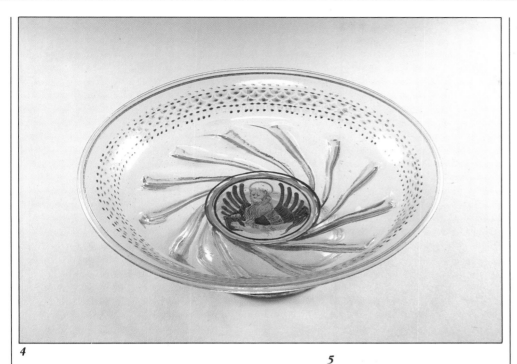

4

6

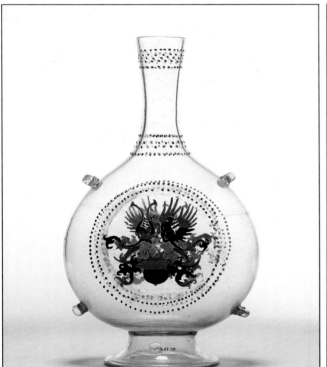

5

7

4 *A clear glass tazza, made c.1500, resting on a low foot, with gilt and enamel scale pattern. The central medallion depicts the lion of St Mark.*

5 *Pilgrim's flasks were made in metal, pottery and glass. This example dates from the first quarter of the sixteenth century, and is enamelled with a coat-of-arms on front and back.*

6 *A late fifteenth-century goblet in opaque turquoise-blue glass with a stem of lapis-lazuli blue. Only two other similar glasses of this date are known.*

7 *The stem of this sixteenth-century tazza in clear glass has a gilded knop of lions' heads alternating with cartouches. On the underside of the bowl a disc of clear glass has been laid over the enamelled coat of arms, a revival of the sandwich glass technique used by the ancient Romans.*

VENETIAN UNCOLOURED

1,2 Cristallo *glass, produced by adding lime to the soda-silica mix, was much purer, thinner and brighter than anything used before, and gave the Venetian glassmakers a chance to exploit their skill in blowing. This exuberant tazza and jug, and the delightful goblets with trailed-on blue-glass handles, testify to their delight in the new "metal".*

3 *Two goblets with bowls made in* vetro a filigrana, *a technique of embedding white canes in the glass. Both date from the second half of the sixteenth century.*

4 *A sixteenth-century vase with a stylized pattern of foliage engraved in diamond point.*

5 *A mid-sixteenth-century sprinkler in* vetro a filigrano. *This may have been made for export, as the shape is common in the Middle East.*

6 *Where the canes of glass are twisted to form spirals, as on this sixteenth-century cup and cover, the technique is known as* vetro a retorti.

7 *A group of sixteenth-century wine glasses in* cristallo *glass.*

8 *This footed bowl is in ice glass, made in large quantities for export, and particularly prized by Philip II of Spain.*

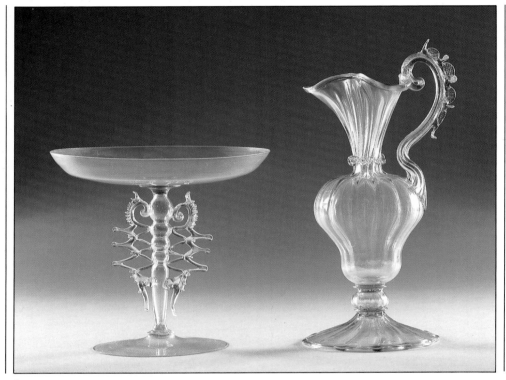

1

2

3

4

5

6

7

8

VENETIAN COLOURED

3,5 *These miniature ewers, dating from the early sixteenth century, are made of* millefiori glass, *one of several ancient Roman techniques revived by the Venetians. Such vessels are rare, and were apparently not made in great numbers – they may have been collectors' "curiosities".*

4 *Another rarity is chalcedony glass, marbled to give the effect of natural hardstones. This vase is an early example of the technique (it was made c.1500), and demonstrates the breathtaking skill of the glassmakers.*

6 *In the seventeenth and eighteenth centuries Venetian glass became increasingly elaborate. This covered jug, made c.1700, has a combed pattern of white threads and applied patterns on the body, while the top of the cover takes the form of an opening bud with pointed petals of blue and white glass. A set of similar combed glass was presented to King Frederick IV of Denmark in 1709.*

1

2

1 *The elegant shapes of these vases in emerald-green glass are superbly complemented by the elaborate gilt mounts. "Gem mania" had reached its peak in Europe by the seventeenth century, when these were made, and the Murano glassmakers vied with one another to produced imitations of the precious and semi-precious stones so avidly collected by their princely patrons.*

2 *This lovely amethyst-coloured goblet dating from the late sixteenth century is moulded with bands enclosing lozenges, a type of decoration known as "nipt diamond waies" – this phrase appeared in the price list of the great British glassmaker George Ravenscroft.*

3

4

5

6

FAÇON DE VENISE

1

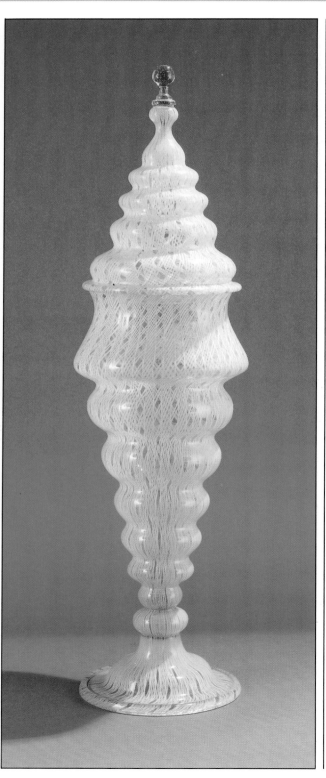

2

1 This extremely rare goblet dated 1586 was made in the London glasshouse of Jacopo Verzelini, who had been granted a Royal Patent in 1574 and was the only person allowed to make Venetian-style glass in England. It might have been engraved by a Frenchman called Anthony de Lysle, who was living in London then. It has the initials GS twice joined by a lover's knot – perhaps a marriage goblet? It is also engraved with "In God is al mi trust", which is the motto of the Pewterers Company. There are only ten known glasses attributed to Verzelini, and they bear dates ranging from 1577 to 1590.

2 This large and magnificent goblet and cover is of South Netherlands manufacture and dates from the end of the sixteenth to the beginning of the seventeenth century. The opaque white canes are called vetro a retorti because the canes are twisted to form a variety of patterns. The cover has a clear cristallo finial. Similar glasses were made in Venice and exported to German and North European markets, but many Muranese workers also settled in the Netherlands.

3

3 *This helmet-shaped jug, of Spanish manufacture and probably sixteenth century, is of ice glass, produced by plunging an initial blowing of glass into cold water and then reheating it gently. A final blowing is then done, which enlarges the tiny cracks and gives the glass a sparkling, frosted appearance.*

5

4

4 *A façon de Venise goblet and cover probably made at Innsbruck in the Tyrol c. 1570-90. This glasshouse was founded by Archduke Ferdinand II after he left Prague in 1563, and was staffed by Venetian glassmakers. A plate in the British Museum has similar diamond point engraving with traces of gilding and cold painting, as this has.*

5 *A decidedly Spanish shaped eighteenth-century cantir, probably from a Catalan glasshouse, with decoration in Venetian* vetro a fili *style. This was probably achieved by lining the sides of a mould with plain opaque white canes alternating with clear ones, which became attached to the gather of clear glass before it was inserted into the mould. The glassmaker could then "marver" the canes into the surface. The blue glass decoration would be trailed or applied to the finished vessel.*

ROEMERS AND WALDGLAS

1

3

2

1 An unusually large roemer, of the green-tinted glass known as waldglas or forest glass, with a hollow stem decorated with four well-controlled rows of prunts. This type of glass was for long the typical one used for Rhenish white wine. It was made in the early seventeenth century.

2 This green-glass beaker is called a krautstrunk (or cabbage-stem) glass, and also has rows of prunts as decoration. It is much earlier than (**1**), dating from the end of the fifteenth to the beginning of the sixteenth century, but the same type, with variations, was made in Germany and the Netherlands for over 200 years.

3 This flask is of a rare form which was introduced in the fifteenth century; few examples survive, although there is one in the Victoria and Albert Museum, London. Similar vessels appear in a "recipe" book in the library at Weimar, copied from a manuscript of 1430.

5

4 *A German* daumenglas *in colourless glass, dating from the seventeenth century. This type has indentations or thumbpieces to give the drinker an extra hold on the glass.*

5 *A German thick-walled tumbler, dated 1659, of very dark green glass. It has a couplet engraved in diamond point exhorting the spectator to join in the drinking. A number of similar glasses is known, bearing the same inscription but dating from the 1640s to the 1660s.*

4

ROEMERS AND WALDGLAS

1

1 *German or Netherlandish passglas – popularly said to be so called because it was passed around the assembled company, with each member drinking down to the next ring or marker. It is extremely difficult to distinguish between the glass of the Low Countries and that from the Lower Rhineland at this time.*

2 *The applied prunts on this Bohemian blue-glass tankard, also dating from the seventeenth century, are a type known as raspberry prunts, which came back into fashion in the nineteenth century as a method of decoration.*

2

3 Two Netherlandish or Rhenish roemers of late seventeenth-century date, showing the taller stem and high-spun conical foot. Such glasses are commonly seen in Dutch still-life pictures of the period. The meaning of the word roemer *is disputed – it may be derived from the Lower Rhenish word* roemen *(to boast) – in this case perhaps of how much one could drink.*

3

1

2 A Bakers' Guild humpen, with the arms of the guild painted on one side together with the date 1664. The reverse has an inscripton stating that the glass belonged to Michel Hoffman, who was a baker in the town of Freiburg.

3 This large beer humpen from Franconia is a type known as an Ochsenkopfhumpen because it is painted with a stylized depiction of the mountain of that name. The mountain was traditionally associated with hidden mineral wealth, and the inscription refers to gold, silver, pewter and copper. This example is dated 1699, but these vessels were made from the mid-seventeenth century, painted with symbols that refer to the fertility of the region.

2

3

1 This humpen, or large beer beaker, is dated 1651 and is painted in bright enamel colours with The Crucifixion on top of the Imperial double-headed eagle. On the wings are the coats of arms of a hierarchy of the Holy Roman Empire, which start with the "Potestat" of Rome and then go on to the spiritual and temporal electors. Popular prints from the end of the fifteenth century depict these also, and a woodcut of 1511 appears to be the inspiration for the version used by the glass painters.

4 A Saxon enamelled passglas with three main zones, the top painted in white with a taler (a coin) with a portrait of Johann Georg, Duke of Saxony. The centre shows a large red lobster, and at the bottom there is a figure of a man in early eighteenth-century costume – the date of the glass itself. The Saxon glasses are distinctive for their bright clear glass and the fresh tones of their enamels.

5 This Saxon passglas is of the type known as hofkellerei which were made for the Saxon Court residences. This example bears the arms of Saxony surmounted by an Elector's hat, below the word "Vivat". The glass dates from the end of the seventeenth century and many are known with dates in the 1680s, also with the arms of the Electors of Saxony.

1

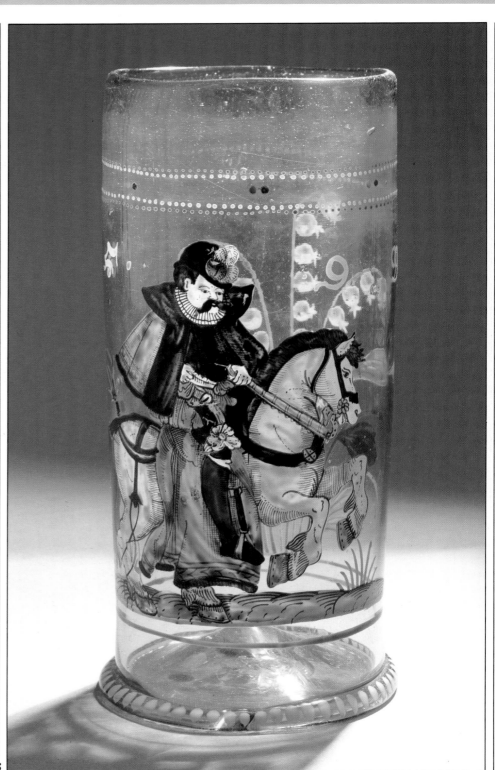

2

3

4

5

1 The Sacrifice of Isaac is the subject depicted on this Saxon tankard dated 1758, and the inscription notes that it has been taken from the Book of Moses, verses 11 and 12. Tankards of this type are well known also in German pottery, and the pewter mounts are also typical.

2 This guild humpen is typical of the robust peasant art found on such glasses. It is painted with the arms of the Guild of Butchers below an inscription, while the reverse shows a butcher with an axe about to kill a calf tethered to a column. It is inscribed with the name "Christian Bloger" – probably the name of the butcher who might have presented it to his guild, and is dated 1676.

3 A Bohemian humpen painted with an elaborately dressed horseman flanked by the date 1599 and a spray of lilies-of-the-valley. The rider is taken from a print by Jost Amman from the 1584 edition of Kunstreiche Figuren zu der Reutterey.

4 This tankard is enamelled with the arms of von Wirsberg and von Schwanberg, their initials G.C.V.W. and V.W.G. V.S. and the date 1614. It is probably of Bohemian or Franconian origin – the latter often having white dotted borders, as seen here. The stoneware of this area is decorated in the same way.

5 This amusing beaker dated 1696 is painted in white and black and depicts the popular Ages of Man – ten in this instance. Each of the ten couples age by ten years (from "10 years as a child" to "100 years old"), and each is accompanied by a rhyme, which might have been taken from Agricola's collection of rhymes of 1528.

SCHWARTZLOT ENAMELLING

1 *This Nuremberg goblet with its typical hollow-knopped stem was painted in the* schwarzlot, *or black enamel, technique by Johann Ludwig Faber. The scenes are taken from engravings in Matthaus Merian's* Emblemata Moralia et Bellica *of 1615 and the glass can be dated to the end of the seventeenth century. Faber also painted on faience and window glass.*

2 *A Nuremberg tumbler attractively painted with a hunting scene in* schwarzlot *and coloured enamels, possibly by a follower of Johann Schaper.*

3 *This* roemer *painted in* schwarzlot *with a border of sailing ships is very similar to one in the Victoria and Albert Museum, London, which is finely painted with* putti *in shell boats drawn by seahorses. Both these glasses may be Netherlandish rather than German and probably should be dated to the beginning of the eighteenth century.*

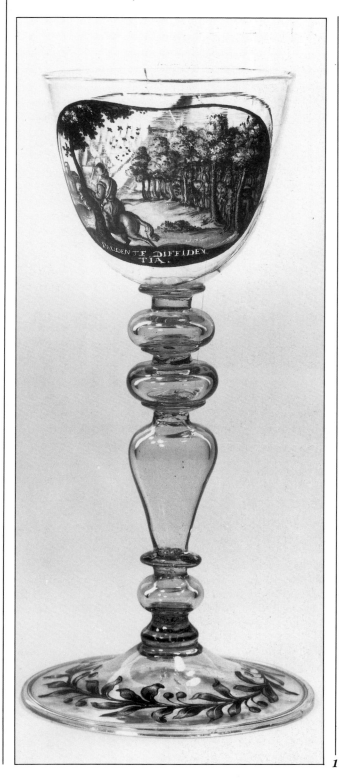

1

2

ENGRAVING

4 Hermann Schwinger engraved this Nuremberg goblet, which bears a half-length portrait of Paul Albrecht Rieter on one side, his coat-of-arms on the reverse, and an inscription in elaborate calligraphy, signed JBH, on the stem. Rieter, an official of the Nuremberg Council, was obviously a gentleman of some importance who felt that he merited a fine glass with his portrait on it.

5 This cylindrical shape on three bun feet is typical of Nuremberg beakers. This example, dating from the late seventeenth century, is engraved with a shore battery on one side and a ship on the reverse.

6 Hermann Schwinger was again the engraver of this armorial tumbler bearing the coat-of-arms of the Nuremberg family of Krauss within finely engraved palm fronds tied with a ribbon bow. The reverse has a scene of Jacob wrestling with the angel, taken from an engraving by Matthaus Merian.

4

5

6

Eighteenth-century English wine glass, grog glass and goblet, cut and wheel engraved.

CHAPTER · THREE
THE 17th AND 18th CENTURIES

THE 17th AND 18th CENTURIES

The emerging style of the German-speaking lands in the period after the Thirty Years War produced two distinct trends. The first was the technique of enamelling on glass discussed in the previous chapter, and the second was a great flowering of glass engraving. It started at the beginning of the seventeenth century in Prague and then in Nuremberg, on thin-blown glass in Venetian style, but this was too brittle for deep engraving. The discovery in the last quarter of the century of a new type of potash glass, made by the addition of lime and chalk, was to transform the "metal", as it is usually called, into a less fragile material capable of supporting lapidary-style engraving.

In late-Renaissance Europe there was a great interest in the engraving of precious stones, as there had been in Roman times, and they were collected by the princely courts of Europe. In 1588 one Casper Lehmann was appointed official gem cutter to the court of Rudolf II in Prague, and he was the first European artist to use the lapidary's wheel for engraving glass, usually working on flat plaques rather than hollow vessels.

When Lehmann died, in 1622, he bequeathed his privilege for crystal and glass engraving to a pupil, Georg Schwanhardt, a Nuremberger, who returned to his native city taking this concession with him. There are several known glasses signed by Schwanhardt, which show a mastery of wheel engraving, supplemented with delicate diamond point.

Schwanhardt's two sons, Georg the Younger (d 1676) and Heinrich (c. 1693), and three of his daughters were all glass engravers. Others from the same city were Hermann Schwinger (1640-1683), who is probably best known for his portrait goblets; and a slightly later artist, Georg Friedrich Killinger (d 1726), who engraved fine land-scapes. Johann Wolfgang Schmidt, another fine portrait engraver, also excelled in depicting well-known battle scenes, both at sea and on land.

The golden age of glass-engraving

The above-named artists are only the known exponents of a widespread production which lasted nearly a hundred years. The Treaty of Utrecht in 1713 began a rare period of relative tranquillity in Europe, and the glass industry was encouraged by German courts, some of whom set up workshops for the artists in their employ.

The first was in Petersdorf in Silesia, where in 1687 Count Christoph Leopold von Schaffgotsch gave Friedrich Winter a privilege "for engraving glass in the manner of crystal". In 1690-1 Winter set up a water-power mill to engrave glasses in the difficult *hochschnitt* (cameo relief) style, which are very obviously inspired by carvings in rock crystal and other semi-precious stone. In 1687 Friedrich's brother Martin set up an engraving workshop

Right A Franconian tankard in white (or milchglas*) decorated in black enamel (*schwarzlot*) with two stags running towards a spring and mounted with a magnificent silver-gilt cover. It is inscribed beneath the handle with two lines from Psalm 42 and dated "Anno Domini 1685".*

Below A Potsdam or Zechlin goblet and cover with a drawn funnel bowl, decorated with cut and gilt arched facets on the stem, the cover with large ring knop. The glasshouse at Potsdam was set up in 1679 but was moved to Zechlin in 1736 – it remained as a state concern until 1890.

in Berlin. He had been patronized for several years by the Elector of Brandenburg, and he had a very gifted nephew and pupil called Gottfried Spiller who became his partner in 1683. They also had a water-power mill for the *hochschnitt* technique, but also produced the more usual *tiefschnitt*, or intaglio work, in association with the Potsdam glasshouse which actually made the glasses.

The Bohemian-Silesian area had a great glass engraving industry, and its productions were eventually exported not only to every part of Europe but also to Persia and the East. It is difficult to differentiate Bohemian glass from Silesian, but as far as the finest engraving is concerned the Bohemian workshops were predominant in the late seventeenth and early eighteenth centuries, giving place to those of Silesia about 1725.

The styles of the Bohemian engravers fall into an easy sequence. From about 1700, and for nearly twenty years, the surface of the glass was covered with a formal design of small flowers and foliage. Towards 1720 the style, although still formal, began to include Baroque strapwork and Chinoiseries in the manner of prints by Paul Decker, J. L. Eysler and J. C. Rieff, whose designs were sometimes directly copied. Many of the polygonal or faceted tumblers of this period are very finely engraved, but some are quite crude; it may be that the best examples were the work of

engravers, the Sangs. Their fame was such that Andreas Friedrich Sang was appointed glassmaker to the Saxon court in 1738, while Johann Balthasar Sang worked for that of Brunswick. The third, Jacob Sang, is known by signed glasses engraved by him in Holland.

Dutch engraved glass

As far as shapes were concerned, most seventeenth-century Dutch glass was a reflection of German glass, but there were important differences in the decoration. Diamond point engraving inspired by Venetian styles was practised, but it was not a product of the glasshouses or a professional workshop; its exponents were mostly amateurs who engraved as a hobby. One of the first was Anna Roemers Vischer (1587-1651), who engraved flowers, insects and fruit, copied from prints of contemporary Dutch paintings, and another was Willem van Heemskerk (1613-92). A brilliant amateur engraver, he was a cloth merchant by trade, but also wrote plays and poetry. He used both diamond point and wheel engraving, and is best known for his calligraphic treatment of mottoes and biblical quotations, usually on coloured glass bottles or jugs.

By the middle of the eighteenth century the German fashion of wheel engraving had become popular in Holland. Jacob Sang had established commercial engraving workshops in Amsterdam by the 1750s, and possibly in

Left *A Netherlands green glass roemer dated 1687, the large bowl engraved in diamond point by an artist who signed himself as "G. V. Nes", but of whom nothing else is known. It has the coat-of-arms of William III and of the Seven United Provinces, and the arms are surmounted by a border of very well-drawn flowers.*

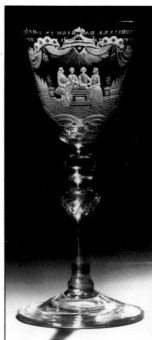

independent engravers or those working for a court, while the others were done in the glasshouses in a more mass-produced way.

The Silesian glass is Rococo in style, and popular forms were lobed goblets and shell-shaped cups, based on silver and gold objects. Some have gem-like miniature engravings, others allegorical figures, views and armorial bearings. Many of the later designs were also copied from prints – by such Augsburg designers as J. W. Baumgartner and J. E. Nilsson. Unfortunately few of the engravers' identities are known, although some of the finest work in the mid-century was done by a Warmbrunn artist called Christian Gottfried Schneider, who engraved elaborate allegorical designs.

Much engraving was also done in Thuringia, and from Ilmenau in this area came an extremely gifted family of

Above *An English "Newcastle" wine glass engraved in Holland by J. Sang, and signed by him. It showns a scene of four people at an altar-like stand, enclosed by elaborate scrolls and a crown-like pediment. The elegant stem has a shoulder knop containing "tears".*

Right *A Netherlands clear glass flask engraved in diamond point and attributed to Willem Moorleyser. It shows a shepherd and shepherdess on one side, and on the other is a boy playing a flute and a girl with a tambourine.*

other Dutch towns as well. The engravers used English glasses, mostly of Newcastle manufacture, and produced finely worked allegorical and armorial subjects and also glasses with ships of the Dutch East India Company – showing the rise of a new kind of patron.

At much the same time a revival of diamond point became popular in the form of stippling, a uniquely Dutch technique in which the diamond is used to create a picture in dots rather than lines. One of the finest stipple-engravers was Frans Greenwood (1680-1761), a native of Rotterdam, possibly of English parentage. He worked for the municipality of Dordrecht, but practised glass decorating as a hobby, normally using English baluster glasses, onto which he copied prints of contemporary paintings. A follower and possible pupil of Greenwood was a professional artist named Aert Schouman, and other known exponents of the style were G. H. Hoolart and J. van den Blijk, working mainly in the 1770s.

English lead glass

It took most of the seventeenth century for the English glass industry to move from the Venetian style of Verzelini (see Chapter Two) to the English style, in which the distinctive lead glass was used. In 1615, Sir Robert Mansell obtained a patent to manufacture all kinds of glass, and held the industry in an iron grip for some thirty years. Glassmaking suffered during the upheavals of the Civil War, and in 1660, with the Restoration of Charles II, another monopolist emerged, the Duke of Buckingham. He controlled the industry through patentees, using both Italian and French workmen and also importing glass from Venice, so that it is impossible to distinguish the separate productions.

However, it was the aim of the Glass Sellers Company, which was given a new Charter by Charles II in 1664, to make the English glass industry independent of foreign workers and materials, and in 1673 it engaged George Ravenscroft (1618-81) to research the material in its two glasshouses at Henley on Thames and the Savoy in London. This led to the highly important discovery of English glass-of-lead. It was heavier than the Venetian *cristallo*, and would not blow out so thin, but it had an amazing brilliance and light-dispersing character.

The importance of this new glass was realized immediately: in 1676 Ravenscroft was allowed to use a raven's head seal, and by the end of the seventeenth century a hundred glasshouses over England were using lead glass. The best work was in the area of wineglasses, where the early hollow stems gave way to solid ones, simple and massive as befitted the lead "metal". These were called balusters after the architectural balusters from which they derived their shape, and were in vogue from about 1690 until 1725. Their strength must have also been

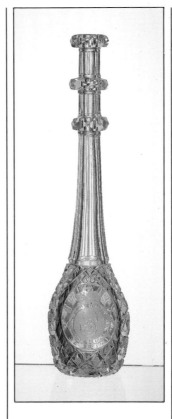

Above A finely cut Regency-style toddy lifter dating from c.1820. It is cut with panels of "strawberry diamonds" and engraved with the initial S for Augustus Frederick, Duke of Sussex. The initial is bordered by the royal motto and surmounted by a coronet.

Right An attractive group of green glass, the decanter labels and initials on the matching pear-shaped stoppers in gilding. Both green and blue glass were popular for decanters and glasses of this period, and the decanters were often in a stand holding three or four.

appreciated by the users of the time, who had rumbustious drinking habits.

The accession in 1714 of the Hanoverian George I as King of England brought German influence, which in glassmaking was seen in a form of a ribbed and shouldered stem, formerly called "Silesian". It is known on glasses which are moulded on the knop, "God Bless King George", no doubt meant as Coronation glasses as they date from about 1714-15. It was also popular on sweetmeat glasses.

About a decade later, the heavy baluster stems gave way to light ones, partly due to the new Rococo style. A much sought-after type is that known as a Newcastle after its supposed place of origin, Newcastle-on-Tyne. Dating from about 1725 onwards, it is tall and graceful, with a knopped stem. English engraving was also done on the light baluster type, although it was never as good as the Dutch and German engraving for which the same glasses were used.

Perhaps some of the most prized engraved glasses are those with Jacobite symbols and inscriptions, usually engraved with the rose and one or two buds, and sometimes in addition a thistle, an oak leaf, a star and various mottoes. A few rare examples bear a portrait of the Prince. (These glasses have been extensively copied – usually using genuine eighteenth-century glasses.) There are also glasses engraved with Williamite and Georgian loyal mottoes, and some rare political and "Privateer" glasses – the latter engraved for the captains and/or owners of the ships which raided French shipping during the Seven Years War (1756-63).

In 1745 a tax was levied on glass, on a weight basis, and heavy, solid stems were no longer economic. Formations changed to plain drawn stems and some hollow ones,

followed by the air twist and opaque colour-twists. The former were made by trapping a pattern of tiny air bubbles in the glass as the stem was drawn, and the latter were a version of the Venetian *vetro a filigrana* (see Chapter Two), made by implanting white or coloured canes in clear glass.

English and Irish cut glass

Cutting was to prove a form of decoration particularly well-suited to English lead glass. It became more and more appreciated both at home and abroad, being preferred to the Bohemian because of its brilliance. The characteristic of the cutting of the latter part of the eighteenth century, seen on glasses, sweetmeats, cruets and some rare decanters, was that it was shallow, which meant that there was little loss of transparency. This style was to continue into the so-called "classical" period at the end of the century and the great age of cut glass in the following one.

Large numbers of eighteenth-century drinking glasses have survived, and it is interesting to note in this connection that there was at the time a wide variety of clubs and societies: One historian claims that every male in Georgian London belonged to a club of some sort. These ranged from benefit clubs for tradesmen and artisans, debating and cultural clubs; purely convivial clubs like the Sublime Society of Beef-steaks (to which Hogarth belonged) and many Masonic and quasi-Masonic clubs. Another important factor is that both the ceramic and glass factories in England were products of private enterprise, whereas the tradition on the Continent, especially in Germany, was one of royal or noble patronage. This meant that in England glass had to be commercially viable, which did not allow for the production of great masterpieces of enamelling and engraving subsidized from a royal exchequer. However, the new prosperity and cultural awareness of the British middle classes provided a different kind of patronage.

The use of cut table glass became common in England by the end of the century. Drinking glasses became shorter, the stems usually having a central blade or ball knop. Matching services of glass were made comprising decanters, claret jugs, finger bowls, wine-glass rinsers, water and cream jugs, tumblers, stands, plates and jelly glasses.

The British also had a virtual monopoly on glass light fittings; earlier, chandeliers and wall sconces had usually been made of ormolu, brass or silver, and were mainly manufactured in France, Holland or Germany. The more prosperous middle class was supplied with many sources of recreation – Londoners had more than sixty "pleasure gardens", and the provincial cities and popular watering places had a growing number of Assembly Rooms. The

Right *A Jacobite wine glass enamelled in colours with a full-face, nearly half-length portrait of the young Pretender, a portrait which is also known on engraved glasses. The battle of Culloden Moor in 1745 and the ignominious flight of the Prince marked the end of Stuart pretension to the throne.*

Assembly Rooms at Bath had, and still have, magnificent chandeliers made by William Parker of Fleet Street, who obtained his glass from the nearby Whitefriars glasshouse. Theatres, too, were spreading to such centres as Birmingham, Bristol and Norwich, increasing the market for glass, both for drinking and lighting.

The Irish were to develop a particularly national idiom both in chandeliers and glass vessels, including large bowls with turnover rims, jugs, piggins (handled bowls to hold cream) and blown decanters, often with the name of the glasshouse impressed on the base. The increased duty on glass imposed by Acts of 1777, 1781 and 1787 in England had the effect of boosting the manufacture of glass in Ireland, where there was no excise duty at all. This was further enhanced by the granting in 1780 of Free Trade between Ireland and England, and glasshouses were started in Dublin, Cork, Belfast and Waterford.

INSPIRATIONS

Throughout history there has been a constant interchange of ideas between the fine and applied arts, and both ceramists and glassmakers drew on paintings and prints, metalwork and jewellery for their ideas. The style of detailed topographical painting popular in the eighteenth century and seen in this view of the orangerie at Versailles by Pierre Denis Martin (*1*) reappears in the finely engraved glass of the German and Bohemian artists of the period.

The Lute Player *by Van Mieris. Detail of (*2*). Dutch glassware is seen in many of the seventeenth- and eigtheenth-century genre paintings, and the influence was a two-way one, as glass engravers took themes from contemporary paintings as their subject matter.*

1

2

3

From early times glass had been influenced by metalwork, and during the seventeenth and eighteenth centuries the kind of heroic scenes and lavish decoration used on this silver-gilt plate (*3*) were seen on the grand and expensive glass vessels made for royalty and the nobility.

4

5

Traditional metalwork shapes (4) were also used for glass vessels, not surprisingly, since both served the same purpose, and many glass goblets echo the outlines of this silver cup and cover made c. 1578.

The ancient art of carving hardstones was revived in the Renaissance, and led to the development of glass engraving, for which the same lapidary wheel was used – the first European glass engraver was the gem cutter at the court of Rudolf II at Prague. This sardonyx cameo (5) was given to the Medici Pope, Clement VII, by the Emperor Charles V.

ROYAL GOBLETS

2

1 *A very large Potsdam goblet and cover made c. 1713, engraved with the arms of Hanover and Brandenburg beneath a crown on one side, and the reverse with crowned initials. The knobs on the cover and stem have been finely matt-engraved with leaf motifs imitating borders found on gold goblets.*

2 *This goblet carries the monogram FA, for Frederick Augustus I of Saxony, and bears the arms of Saxony. One can see the crossed swords which were later to be used by the famous porcelain factory of Meissen.*

3 *This finely engraved goblet and cover is attributed to the Master H.I. – probably Heinrich Jäger who worked at Potsdam with Gottfried Spiller. It has an inscription and three crowns – referring to the royal arms of Sweden – and is engraved with figures of Hercules and Mars, symbolizing strength and war, and Ceres and Bacchus symbolizing plenty (bread and wine).*

1

3

5

4 *Another large goblet and cover, this one made by Gottfried Spiller c. 1688-1701. It has polished matt and deep engraving, showing the arms of Frederick III, Elector of Brandenburg, beneath a royal crown and panels with the monogram also surmounted by a crown.*

5 *Also of impressive size, this goblet and cover is probably from Brunswick or Hessen. The bowl is engraved with the initials AW (for August Wilhelm von Braunschweig-Wolfenbüttel) on one side. The reverse is engraved with the Brunswick horse.*

6 *A Saxon amber-tinted marriage goblet engraved with the arms of Reuss, probably for the marriage of Count Heinrich Reuss and Conradine Eleonore Isabella on the 4th April 1743.*

4

6

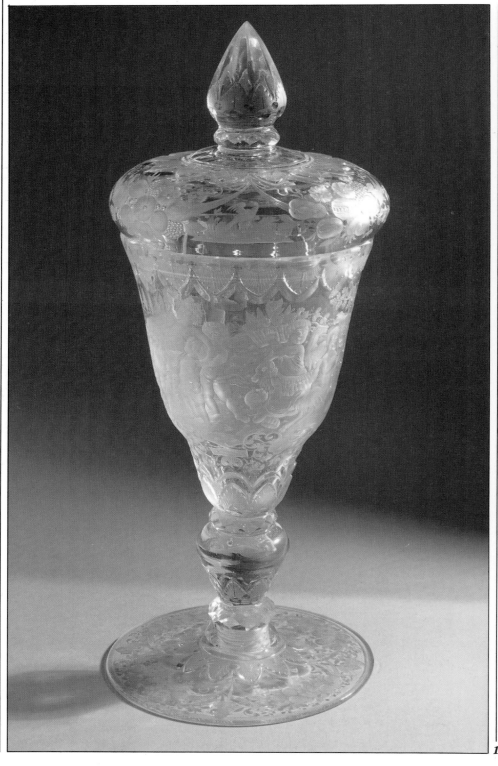

3

1 *A finely engraved goblet and cover by Friedrich Winter, with Bacchic scenes after engravings by Pieter van Avont after Wenzel Hollar. This is a masterpiece of engraving, in which the artist has covered the entire surface of the glass.*

2 *A Silesian goblet and cover dated 5 December 1757, most minutely engraved with a depiction of the Battle of Leuthen and a portrait of Frederick the Great. The battle, at which Frederick defeated the Austrians against a vastly superior force, took place in November of that year· so great were the odds against Frederick that the story goes that he called his generals together before the battle and offered them the opportunity not to fight with him.*

3 *This goblet, like the example on page 80, is attributed to the Master H.I. – Heinrich Jäger – and dates to the first quarter of the eighteenth century. It is strongly engraved in both matt and polished techniques. The well-balanced inverted baluster stem was also popular in early eighteenth-century English glasses.*

4

5

4 *This is another finely engraved goblet attributed to Friedrich Winter or his workshop, with the crest of the Schaffgotsch family and their motto. Winter was granted a special privilege by Count Christian von Schaffgotsch in 1687 to set up a water-powered cutting works.*

5 *A Silesian goblet attributed to C.G. Schneider of Warmbrunn, and engraved with a continuous Bacchanalian scene celebrating the grape harvest, with one boy riding a goat and others playing musical instruments. The engraving is very detailed and of the highest quality.*

2

1 A tall-stemmed roemer diamond engraved by Willem Mooleyser, signed and dated 1685, which is an early date for this artist. The scene of dancing peasants is reminiscent of Dutch painters such as Brueghel and Steen.

2 The bowl of this well-proportioned English wine glass, dating to about 1760, was engraved in Holland by Jacob Sang and signed "J. Sang". The ship is engraved in great detail, while the reverse shows a farmer, horse and plough.

1

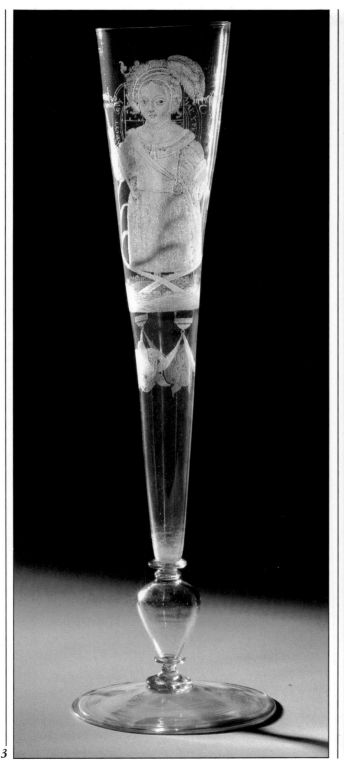

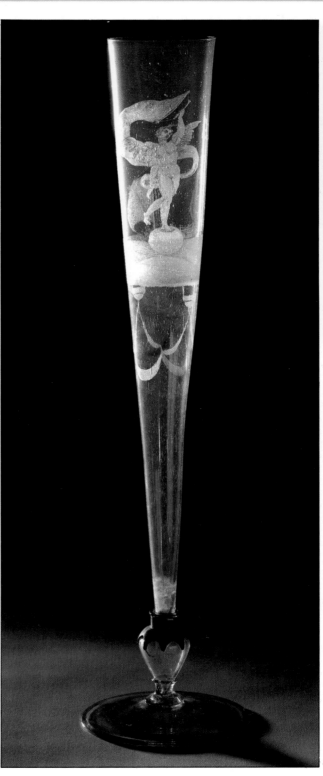

5

3 A Netherlands flute engraved in diamond point by the monogramist M, with a three-quarter length portrait of the three-year-old Prince William III of Orange, later William III of England. It is signed "fc M" and dated 1657.

4 Another flute, signed by the same engraver and dated 1662. It is decorated with a winged figure of Fortune standing on a globe, the reverse with a "man-of-war".

5 This Newcastle goblet is stipple-engraved, a technique peculiar to the Netherlands, in which the point of the diamond is used to make countless minute dots.

3

4

ZWISCHENGOLDGLAS

1 *Zwischengoldglas is a technique of sealing gold and enamel decoration between two layers of clear glass, a revival of the sandwich glass technique used in ancient Rome. The wine glass at left has a small circular zwischengold medallion while the remainder of the bowl is engraved with foliate scrolls, which is an unusual combination of techniques. The central medallion of the flask depicts St John Nepomuk; it is sometimes suggested that this type of decoration was done in a workshop either in or connected with a monastery in Bohemia, and views of monasteries and Bohemian saints are found as motifs.*

2 *The small tumbler on the left of the group is a rare variation of the technique. The sides are faceted and the outside is painted in pink, orange and dark brown with gilt veining to simulate marble, while the inside is gilt. The other pieces are decorated with scenes of fashionable life: hunting – a popular theme into the nineteenth century – and an outdoor entertainment with a quartet supplying the music.*

3 *These three zwischengold tumblers are by Johann Mildner of Gutenbrunn, the left and centre examples being signed by him and the first one dated 1792. The tumbler at right has a portrait of St Susanna inscribed on a ruby foil ground, and on the reverse is a short verse which refers to a mother and child, suggesting that the glass may have been for a christening.*

4 *A Silesian* zwischengold *silhouette glass by Johann Sigismund Menzel of Warmbrunn, the oval panel with a silhouette profile bust of a man. Such glasses, like Mildner's work, were probably intended as gifts.*

5 *These three flasks or decanters are also by Mildner. The example at left bears the arms of the Furnberg family: Joseph von Furnberg was Mildner's patron. The base also has a medallion decorated with a circular view of the Furnberg castle, Schloss Lubereck, with logs being floated down-river in front of it.*

3

4

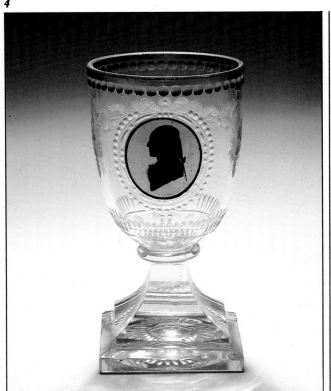

5

EARLY ENGLISH

1

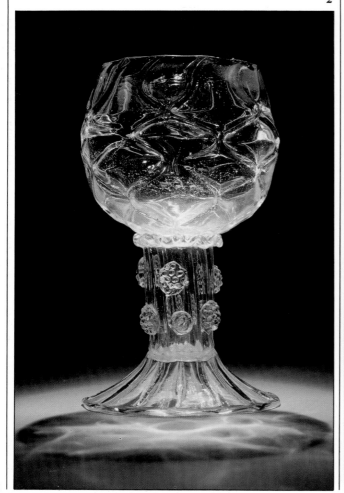

2

3

1 The Butler Buggin bowl is so-called because it bears the arms of Butler Buggin, engraved in diamond point. It is attributed to the Savoy Glasshouse of George Ravenscroft who was the official glassmaker to the Glass Sellers Company from 1674. Although this bowl is of the new lead glass developed by Ravenscroft it shows considerable Venetian influence in its decoration.

2 A version of the German roemer in colourless lead glass. One of the raspberry prunts on the ribbed stem has been replaced by the seal of the raven's head, which Ravenscroft had been allowed to use since 1676 to mark the success of the new glass. The bowl has thick trailed threads pincered into a net design, perhaps the "nipt diamond waies" design referred to by Ravenscroft in his price list of 1677.

3 Another roemer-style glass, with both foot and bowl strongly ribbed, and a frill collar below the bowl. The stem also has **raspberry** prunts and one pad bears the raven's head seal. An imposing jug and a bowl and cover, both in the Victoria and Albert Museum, also show this vertical ribbing.

4 This very simple but fine goblet and cover dates from the last years of the seventeenth century. The plain forms made in silver at this time, encouraged by the softer "Britannia" standard (which was compulsory from 1697 to 1718) may well have influenced the style of this goblet.

4

1

2

3

4

The two decanters (**1**, **4**) and two large wine glasses (**3**) are the work of William Beilby, one of a gifted family working in Newcastle upon Tyne. Enamelling was little practised in England, but Ralph Beilby, William's brother, was a jeweller, silversmith and heraldic engraver, and William had learned the art of enamelling in Birmingham.

2 These small bottles, almost miniature decanters, were held in stands either of silver, silver plate or lacquered papier-mâché. This dark blue glass is often known as "Bristol blue" as a generic term, but although some was made in Bristol it was certainly produced in other centres as well.

5 A rare seventeenth-century wine bottle of English manufacture, probably made at Ravenscroft's Savoy Glasshouse – it has the type of pincered decoration described by Ravenscroft as "nipt diamond waies". The colour was produced by adding the metallic oxide of manganese to the mix. The shape is well known in the Netherlands, where similar bottles were made in blue, green and amber as well as purple.

6 By contrast the blue glass salt-cellar has a distinct English character. It probably dates from about 1790-1800. The British appreciated plain and simple glass, but it is known that cut glass was also produced in the early decades of the eighteenth century: a Jerome Johnson of London advertised "Scalop'd Desert Glasses in the newest fashion" in 1737.

6

5

WINE GLASSES

2

1 A method of dating glasses according to their stem type has now become accepted. Generally speaking, it is as follows. Baluster 1685-1725; pedestal 1715-65; balustroid 1725-55; composite, plain straight and air twist 1740-70; opaque twist 1750-80; mixed and colour twist 1755-75; faceted 1760-1800; short or rudimentary (dwarf ales, jellies etc) eighteenth to nineteenth century. In the illustration above, the stems are, from left to right: yellow opaque twist (rare); blue opaque twist; light baluster; opaque twist; colour-twist thread with red enclosed by opaque twist.

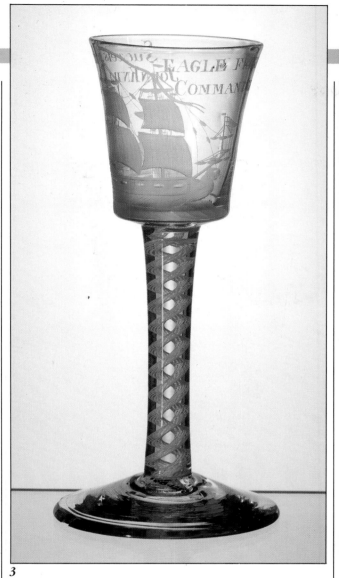

3

4

5

6

2 These are all Jacobite glasses; that on the left is a jelly glass (rudimentary stem). The other are, from left to right: plain; composite with plain section set in a beaded knop; multi-ply air twist with shoulder knops at base; fine multiply air twist.

3 A wheel engraved glass with an opaque twist stem, showing a three-masted ship and inscribed "Success to the Eagle Frigate John Knill Commander". It was made in Bristol in the second half of the eighteenth century.

4 A selection of mixed and colour-twist stems. The examples on left and right have an inner core of lace twist enclosed by spiralling threads of colour.

5 Jacobite glasses. Stems are, from left to right: two plain air twists; combined twist; multi-knopped opaque twist; air twist with swelling knop.

6 Stems are, from left to right: baluster with cusp knop; moulded pedestal; baluster; light baluster; light baluster with shoulder and basal knops.

1

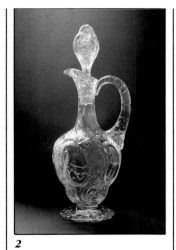

2

1 *The finely engraved and cut decanter and two glasses are from a service made for the Prince Regent – later George IV – about 1810-20. They are engraved with the Prince of Wales' plumes, and the decanter is cut with spiralling panels of diamonds above horizontal bands of hobnail diamonds. The protruding flange on the glasses has a strong Central European feeling.*

2 *Very different in feeling is this elegant claret jug dating from c.1890 and engraved by William Fritsche in the "rock crystal" style. Fritsche was an immigrant Bohemian engraver who set up his own workshop in the Thomas Webb factory and excelled in this technique, which was produced throughout the 1880s and 1890s. He often signed and dated his work. The engraving is deep and covers almost the whole surface, with the engraved lines and areas being polished.*

3

4

3 *This group of decanters shows an interesting range, from the early to the late nineteenth century. The horizontal bands of cutting gave way later to vertical arrangement and to globular decanters with tall necks cut with shallow hollows, or "printies". There are also a few examples of mould-blown decanters.*

4 *The vertical facets on the bodies of these decanters, and the deep bands of prismatic cutting on the shoulders, would have reflected light beautifully. They date from the 1820s and 1830s, and the jug has the massive handle usual at this period – unfortunately often a weak point as the weight on the junction can cause the glass to crack.*

1

2

3

4

5

1 A lovely Neoclassical épergne with shallow dishes for sweetmeats and vase-shaped condiment bottles with silver mounts. All are held in a splendid silver stand of elegant Adam shape. The piece was made in Dublin, and is hallmarked 1787.

2 The cutting on this wine cooler, cover and stand is typical of the Regency period – plain diamonds formed by parallel cutting at ninety degrees. It dates from about 1815, and it falls into the group sometimes called Anglo-Irish – between 1780 and 1825, when several English glassmakers moved to Ireland to avoid the Excise Duty on English glass.

3 The English sweetmeat glass was made c.1785. These often stood in the middle of the top stand of a pyramid of glass tazzas. The author Hannah Glasse in her book The Complete Confectioner (1742) writes "In the middle a high pyramid of one salver above another – these salvers are to be filled with all kinds of wet and dry sweetmeats."

4 A claret jug, probably made in Waterford c.1810, with faceted cylindrical body, a high protruding lip and a typical stout handle. Such tough, sturdy vessels must have been essential for the lively and sometimes wild drinking parties of the time.

5 The celery glass, with its deep bowl and fan-cut rim, is probably also of Waterford manufacture. Such glasses may have been part of a table service which included decanters, jugs, bowls, covered jars and salts.

A Viennese beaker, probably by Anton Kothgasser, painted in transparent enamels, c. 1820-30.

CHAPTER·FOUR
THE INDUSTRIAL AGE

THE INDUSTRIAL AGE

In England and Ireland fine cut glass continued to be made in the Regency style at the beginning of the nineteenth century, and had a tremendous effect on the Continent, particularly France. In 1802 the Voneche factory, on the Franco-Belgian border, became an important producer, as did the factory at Baccarat near St Louis in eastern France. An independent decorating establishment called l'Escalier de Cristal, founded in Paris in 1802, used glass from the Voneche factory which they decorated with diamond cutting and elaborate ormolu mounts.

They had a sensational exhibition in Paris in 1819, where they showed ornate vases, candelabra, clocks and furniture. In 1826 the Val St Lambert factory was founded in Belgium and employed English workers to supervise the cutting. Cut glass was also popular in Russia for the first two decades of the century. The Imperial Glassworks in St Petersburg produced massive vases, ewers and urns and also ventured into furniture, making a blue and crystal divan for the Shah of Persia in 1828.

America was not to be outdone, and first had factories in Pittsburgh, one of which was advertising cut glass in 1809. The New England Glass Company was founded in Boston in 1818, and others followed in New York and Philadelphia. As they employed European cutters and copied European models it is impossible to distinguish American products from European.

In 1825 the Irish glass industry became subject to the excise duty from which the English producers had suffered for eighty years. This, coupled with the shrinking of the hitherto lucrative American export market due to the burgeoning of America's own industry, delivered a death blow to Irish glass. By the middle of the century only Waterford was still working, and even that closed in 1851.

Cut glass continued to be made in England, but was out of fashion between the 1850s and the end of the 1870s. This was partly due to the invention of pressed glass in America, first patented in 1829, which made a cheap version of cut glass universally available. It may also have been a symptom of the intellectual revolt typified by John Ruskin's opinion that "all cut glass is barbaric".

There was, however, a revival in the 1880s and 1890s; in America it was called the "brilliant" period, and is particularly associated with the Libbey Glass Company of Toledo. In Britain, too, manufacturers produced designs of great complexity and richness, and cut glass again became the symbol of middle- and upper-class social and material success.

Bohemia: peace and prosperity

After the disruption to trade caused by the Napoleonic wars, the peace of 1815 ushered in a golden age for the Bohemian glass industry. Bohemia was now part of the Austrian Empire, and enjoyed a peaceful interlude until

Above *A tumbler made at the Baccarat factory in Luneville in France. The decoration, a coat-of-arms, is in coloured enamels and supported on gilt foil foliage, and the style of cutting, a broad band of diamonds between spiral flutes, is typical of the Biedermeier period.*

Right *After the Napoleonic wars there was a resumption of travel by the wealthy middle classes, and this, combined with the new taste for ruins and "picturesque" scenery, produced a market for mementos of places visited. The transparentmalerei (transparent enamels) beaker showing the Brandenburg Gate was painted by Samuel Mohn, who lived in Dresden for the latter part of his life. In 1811 he advertised for sale eighteen beakers all with views of cities and with an oak leaf border - the latter was noted as costing an extra 2-4 thalers.*

Opposite page *Dominik Biemann was one of the most talented engravers of the nineteenth century, as demonstrated by this goblet engraved with the Descent from the Cross. Religious and classical subjects, however, were not a major part of his output; he is best known for his fine portrait medallions, landscapes and horse subjects.*

the mid-nineteenth century, when the Empire was threatened by revolution. This period is known as *Biedermeierzeit* ("the age of the solid citizen") and, in other countries, it was a time of middle-class prosperity.

Although in the late eighteenth century the Bohemian factories had followed the fashion for facet-cut glass, the long tradition of engraving was too strong to be ousted, and Bohemian engravers were unequalled in the nineteenth century. We know the names of many of these talented artists, some of whom worked independently. One of the most famous was Dominik Biemann (1800-57), who engraved portraits and landscapes. He worked mainly at Prague but spent "the season" at the spa of Franzensbad, where he worked to the order of rich, private clients. Another, August Bohm (1812-90), travelled extensively not only on the Continent but also to England and America – some of his finest works are complex and highly skilled engravings of battle scenes, often copied from well-known paintings.

Among the best examples of Biedermeier-style glass are the tumblers and beakers painted in transparent enamels from about 1806. Samuel Mohn (1762-1815) was

a porcelain painter from Leipzig and is reputed to be the instigator of this style, known as *transparentmalerei*. His earliest work, usually signed, is on small cylindrical clear-glass beakers. He painted portraits, silhouettes – which were also a popular style of porcelain painting of the time – and views of various cities.

He trained his son Gottlob (1789-1825), who moved to Vienna in 1811. Here he met Anthon Kothgasser (1769-1851), and both men painted glass beakers in this style. They also painted views, including many of Vienna, landscapes, allegorical figures, flowers, insects, music, playing cards and so on, and their work was highly prized and expensive.

Technical advances

Perhaps it is the variety of colour that provides the most lasting impression of nineteenth-century glass. Several glasshouses in Southern Bohemia owned by Count von Buquoy developed and patented a sealing-wax-red glass in 1819 and an opaque black one in 1817, called Hyalith glass. Forms and decoration were in the Classical style of the Wedgwood black-basalt vases, which were very popular at the time.

In Northern Bohemia in 1829 Friedrich Egermann of Blottendorf (1777-1864) patented his invention of strongly coloured glass imitating agate and semi-precious stones which he called Lithyalin. This was to be copied in the 1840s for its colour by the French firm of von Launay, Hautin et Cie in Paris, who made it into elaborate moulded pseudo-Gothic shapes.

Egermann, who was a chemist as well as a glassblower and glass painter, also developed a yellow stain, using silver-chloride, and a copper-ruby one. These stains were brushed onto an already cut piece of glass and, when fixed by firing, gave the impression of solid colour. They were also used in conjunction with engraving, which cut through the thin film of colour. This led to the development of the more expensive cased glass, which involved using two layers of coloured glass and cutting the outer one away in patterns to show the one below.

In 1836 clear glass within two layers of colour was introduced, and a multitude of objects were made in this technique, sometimes with the addition of painting both in colours and gold. It was extensively copied in England, France and America, and the products of the different countries are almost indistinguishable from one another. Two unusual colours were produced in the 1830s by Joseph Riedel in the Isergebirge, using uranium to produce a greenish-yellow and a yellowish-green glass named Annagrün and Annagelb after his wife Anna. In 1838 George Bontemps at Choisy-le-Roi in France was producing uranium glass, and in the 1840s the St Louis factory was using Egermann-style staining.

Another French development, whose manufacture dates from about 1810, was Opaline, a translucent, milky-white glass which "fires" like an opal stone through transmitted light. This could also be coloured in delicate shades by the addition of metallic oxides, and was sometimes painted with flowers and scenes. Inevitably it was copied: the English firm of Richardsons of Stourbridge produced some fine examples in the 1850s. Equally inevitably, a cheaper version was made, often with green or blue edging and snakes, which was used for tableware as well as decorative items.

Even England, the producer of so much finely cut clear glass, could not ignore this demand for colour, and when the excise duty was lifted in 1845, English glassmakers entered the race. By 1849 they were producing coloured rivals to the Bohemian products, and their success can be judged by the amazing range of coloured wares exhibited at the Great Exhibition of 1851 by such firms as Richardsons, Bacchus & Sons and Rice Harris of Birmingham, and Apsley Pellatt of London.

Revival styles

The Great Exhibition, held at the Crystal Palace, which was the first great building made chiefly of glass, was a huge success – it was visited by six million people in the five months it was open. It set an example which was quickly followed, and exhibition going became a part of late nineteenth-century British life.

A direct consequence was that museums and government-sponsored design schools began to teach "good design", with a strong emphasis on Classical models. Jugs, decanters and vases were soon being made based on Greek forms and engraved with figures inspired by the Elgin marbles and Greek vases. This normally involved using mechanical processes to copy models made by an individual artist, and the copies had none of the freshness and vigour of the originals.

The new mass-production techniques meant that glass was available to a much wider market, but there was also a demand for high-quality products, and around the 1860s a number of highly skilled Bohemian engravers were brought to England to work in their own tradition. Some of these craftsmen, among whom were Paul Oppitz, Franz Eisert, Frederick E. King and William Fritsche, worked independently on blanks ordered by retailers, and some moved around the country, but most were connected at some time or other with prestigious firms such as Thomas Webb of Stourbridge, J. B. Millar of Edinburgh and Stevens & Williams of Brierley Hill. They engraved Classical and Renaissance-style subjects, and naturalistic plants and ferns, and their work was exhibited widely.

This beautiful "rock-crystal" style, in which the decoration was engraved deeply into the glass and then polished,

Above From left to right. A small vase with engraved silver-deposit decoration by a Frenchman called Erard working at the Stevens & Williams factory of Brierley Hill. A small "moss agate" vase or lobed jar, probably made by Stevens & Williams c.1888. With its colour streaks and interior crackle it is an effective simulation of the real stone. Another piece by Stevens & Williams in a type of glass known as Silveria.

reached its peak in the 1880s. Gilt designs in Arab style and versions of Syrian enamelling were also copied at this time: Jules Barbe, working at Thomas Webb about the 1880s and '90s, excelled in gilding, while in France Philippe-Joseph Brocard revived the craft of enamelling on glass and made many clever imitations of Syrian glasses and mosque lamps, winning a First Prize at the 1878 Paris Exposition.

Lobmeyr's of Vienna produced both Renaissance-style and enamelled glass, and in Italy Antonio Salviati (1816-1900) started a revival of Venetian Renaissance-style glass, which he exhibited at the London International Exhibition of 1862 and the Paris Exhibition of 1867. He had a great success, and made the Venetian style popular all over Europe – especially in Britain and America. He founded a company in 1866 funded with British capital, and in 1868 opened a showroom in London. His glass was praised by Charles Eastlake in his popular and influential book *Hints on Household Taste*, written in the same year.

The later nineteenth century

The display of Japanese art in the 1862 London International Exhibition created something of a sensation. Japan had been closed to the West from the early eighteenth century until an expedition by Commodore Perry in 1854, which was followed by an avalanche of imports of bronzes, ivories, ceramics, prints and lacquer work into England. The initial response on the part of glass manufacturers was to use "Japanesque" motifs of storks, bamboo and plum blossom as engraved and enamelled decoration, similar to that on the ceramics of the time. Sowerby's, the makers of pressed glass in Britain, patented in 1879 an ivory-coloured glass called Queen's Ivory Ware, and in 1887 Thomas Webb of Stourbridge patented Ivory Cameo, a most ingenious glass on which they enamelled, gilded, engraved, stained and used a marquetry technique. This Oriental interest was to become one of the major

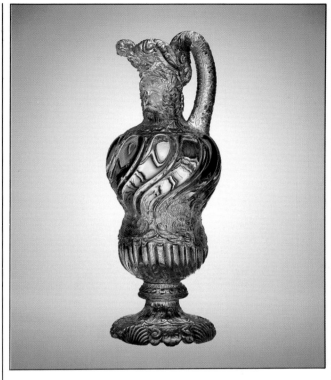

Above left *A "rock crystal" bowl designed by John Northwood and engraved by Frank Scheibner for Stevens & Williams c.1884. Obviously inspired by a Chinese jade or real rock-crystal bowl, it has stylized flowers and relief bosses carved with the Chinese* shou *character for longevity.*

Above right *A "rock crystal" ewer or jug engraved by William Fritsche working at Thomas Webb & Sons. It is signed and dated 1886 and is carved in both high relief and intaglio – a tour-de-force of glass engraving. The waves, shells and fish are full of the movement of water, and the Neptune head on the neck continues the aquatic theme.*

influences on the Art Nouveau style (see Chapter Five).

Perhaps the most important British contribution to nineteenth-century art glass was cameo glass, a revival of the Roman art of the first century AD. It was developed by John Northwood (1836-1902), in response to the offer of a £1000 prize from the Stourbridge manufacturer Benjamin Richardson to the person who first produced an exact replica of the famous Portland vase. Philip Pargeter, owner of the Red House Glassworks in Stourbridge, made the blank, and Northwood devised his own tools for the carving. First he covered the design in acid-resistant varnish, then immersed it in a bath of hydrofluoric acid, and finally chipped away the white glass to reveal the design. Just before the work was finished, the vase cracked and several days later broke in two pieces. Northwood and his assistant glued it together again and finished off the work. It had taken two years.

The achievement brought much publicity, and by about 1880 cameo glass was in great demand and was being produced by Thomas Webb, Stevens & Williams and Richardsons. George Woodall, who started his career in Northwood's workshop, was probably the most gifted of all cameo engravers. His figures of ladies in diaphanous draperies show the most amazing skill.

The introduction of pressed glass had brought both decorative and utilitarian glass within the reach of most people. In America, a vast range of shapes, sizes and colours was made, perhaps one of the best known being "carnival" glass, which had an orange or green iridescence, supposedly imitating Tiffany glass (see Chapter Five), although crudely. France, then Bohemia, Sweden and the other Scandinavian countries followed this lead, and in England the process was first used in Birmingham and Stourbridge, followed by Manchester and then Gateshead and Sunderland in the north.

The final years of the century saw more experimentation with colour, and there was tremendous competition and copying. Heat-sensitive glass was an interesting type which shaded to another colour when a portion of the article was reheated at the furnace – the first was called Amberina, patented by the New England Glass Company in Massachusetts. Peach Blow, Burmese (which was made in America and England) and a great variety of coloured and "satin" glass was also made in England, America and Bohemia.

In a century when there was always a demand for new, colourful and cheap items, a number of real novelties were produced – things such as glass rolling pins, walking sticks, hunting horns, pipes, top hats, glass ships and birds in trees with spun-glass tails. Scent and cologne bottles were popular as mementoes and gifts, and glass paperweights were made in France in the middle of the century, at the great glasshouses of Clichy, Baccarat and nearby St Louis. They revived the Roman technique of *millefiori*, but also produced many beautiful flower weights, and some rare ones with motifs like snakes.

INSPIRATIONS

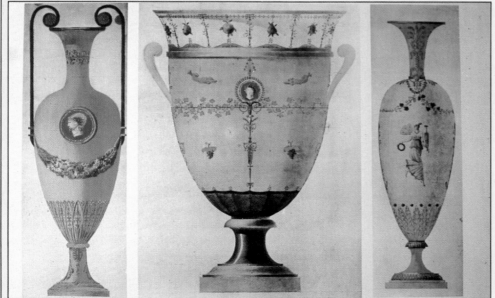

From the 1860s Oriental porcelain began to make an impact on European applied arts. Joshua Hodgetts' wheel-engraved cameo vase (**3**) uses a similar dragon motif to that on the fourteenth-century celadon dish (**1**).

Nineteenth-century style was characterized by an unashamed historicism, but the Classical ideal had already been de rigeur for some time, as demonstrated by these lovely eighteenth-century designs for Sèvres porcelain (**2**).

4

5

6

This soup tureen (**4**) from a service ordered by Ferdinand IV, King of the Two Sicilies, was made c.1781, and inspired by bronzes found at Herculaneum. The influence of the Classical world permeated the eighteenth and nineteenth centuries.

Classical themes like this relief of the Apotheosis of Homer (**5**) appeared on both glass and ceramics, and was particularly well suited to the newly rediscovered art of cameo glass, perfected by the Romans but subsequently lost.

The simple, elegant shapes of Greek vases (**6**) were emulated by some glassmakers, in striking contrast to the extravaganzas of much late-nineteenth-century commercial production.

BOHEMIAN COLOURED

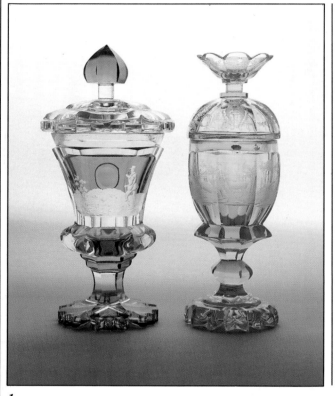

1 The use of colour in Bohemian glass was a reaction to the fashion for clear crystal glass. The engraving of the shooting scene (left) is cut through an amber-flashed panel. The Annagelb goblet (right) is also engraved with hunting motifs – deer and dogs – and the elaborate cover serves as a drinking glass when reversed. Both goblets date from about 1840.

2 This goblet, signed Görner, has a deeply ruby-red bowl encased in clear glass, and the oval medallion is engraved with the Madonna and Child and infant St John (after Raphael).

1

2

3 The gilt and enamelled tumbler (left) is a type known as Annagrün glass. Both this and Annagelb glass were named after the wife of the maker, Josef Riedel. It bears the initials J.W. surrounded by flowers and scrolls in gilding and coloured enamels. The centre beaker is overlaid in ruby red and painted with a border of flowers, while the right-hand example, also with floral painted decoration, is made in a milky glass known as alabasterglas.

3

4 All these goblets have painted and engraved decoration, that on the left on clear glass. The piece in the centre is richly gilded and enamelled with a ruby overlay, while that on the right is clear glass with coloured overlay panels. It is engraved with the names of certain members of a family, and dated 1836.

5 These are examples of the black glass called Hyalith patented by Count Buquoy in 1820. They are gilt with chinoiserie figures.

6 Lithyalin glass, imitating semi-precious and natural stone such as porphyry and marble, was patented in 1829 by Friedrich Egerman.

4

5

6

1 This beaker was made to commemorate Lunardi's balloon ascent of 1791, an event which caused universal interest.

2 The castle of Steyersberg is shown on this goblet painted by the younger Mohn and dated 1816. This type is called "Wildenstein" because Mohn decorated them for the society, "Bund der Wildensteiner Ritterschaft zur blauen Erde".

3 A technique called glasperlein an outer "skin" of coloured glass beads, has been used here, giving the effect of a mosaic picture.

4 This lovely enamel painting, titled "View of the Ketting Bridge near the Rasumovsky Palace in Vienna", has been conjectured to be the work of Anton Kothgasser, although other painters worked in the same style.

3

4

5 A view of Meissen from the banks of the Elbe is the subject of this beaker. The Albrechtsburg castle (where the famous Meissen porcelain was first made) towers above the river and the bridge. The painting was done by Samuel Mohn in the transparentmalerie (or transparent enamels) style, which he is thought to have invented.

5

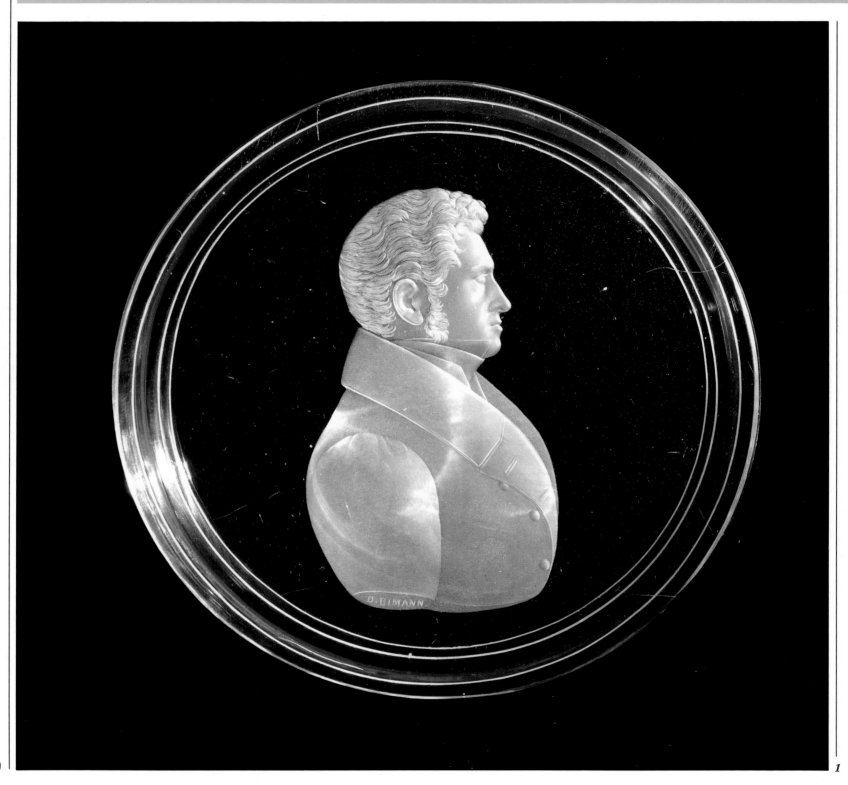

2

3

5

6

4

1 *This fine portrait was engraved by Dominik Biemann of Prague and is signed. We do not know the name of the sitter, but he was probably one of the wealthy visitors to the spa of Franzensbad where Biemann worked in the summers.*

2,5 *The two "sulphide" portraits were made by Pellatt and Green of London. The sitter for (5) is not known, but (2) is a portrait of Rowland Hill, pioneer of the British postal system. Apsley Pellatt obtained a patent in 1831 to produce these suplhides, which he referred to as "crystallo ceramie" in his book* Curiosities of Glassmaking.

3 *A portrait beaker by Dominik Biemann very delicately engraved with a portrait head of a child whose identity is unknown.*

4 *A charming beaker painted in transparent enamels by Gottlob Samuel Mohn and signed. The boy holds a sheet of music, and there is a verse in German which translates as "Remembering the 29th January 1817 from your loving father".*

6 *The French portrait plaque of Napoleon I bears the signature of Deprez, a glassmaker who was working in Paris from the end of the eighteenth century. His "encrusted cameos" were made in a porcelain and glass paste.*

FIGURATIVE

2

1

1 The covered goblet, probably from Lower Austria, is attributed to one Franz Gottstein although it is not signed. It has a finely engraved figure of Pallas Athene with her "familiar", the owl.

3

2 This North Bohemian tumbler is engraved with the Ages of Man going from the "cradle to the grave" in ten-year steps. It was a popular subject often encountered on glass, and the format is usually the same. This example dates to about 1810-20.

3 This cylindrical beaker is attributed to Anton Kothgasser and has the initials AK on the edge of the base. The painting was presumably copied from a print: other examples of the same subject by different painters are known.

4 Austrian transparentmalerei beaker in clear glass with six arched panels, four of which are painted in coloured enamels with a huntsman holding a gun. It dates from about 1830.

4

5 A Viennese flared beaker signed VB and attributed to an artist in the workshop of G.S. Mohn. It dates from c.1814, and shows two young castaways in a small open boat, reminiscent of the story of Paul and Virginia depicted on English ceramics of a slightly later date.

5

ANIMAL MOTIFS

1 This very finely carved Bohemian vase is attributed to Franz Paul Zach. The clear glass is overlaid in cobalt-blue glass, and wheel engraved with four ibex at rest in a forest setting with a range of high mountains in the background.

2 This charming beaker painted by Anton Kothgasser is signed "The painter who lives in the Spanische Spitalberg No. 227 in Vienna." Kothgasser lived in this area from 1804 to about 1820/2, and from 1816 the authorities of the Vienna porcelain factory allowed him to work from his home address (he was also a porcelain painter). The beaker is painted with a black and white dog standing guard over his master's helmet, sword and book and is inscribed "Fidelite".

3 This beaker, also attributed to Kothgasser, is finely painted in transparent enamels with a crowing cockerel – an unusual subject.

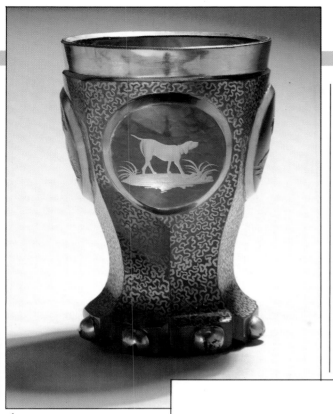

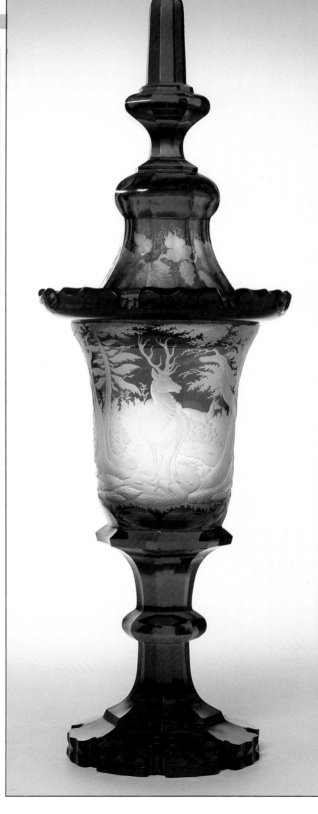

5 *A finely engraved Bohemian goblet with a ruby-stained ground. The stag at bay surrounded by hounds is in the style of August Böhm, who travelled widely and visited both England and America, but the subject is particularly Bohemian in feeling.*

6 *A stag is also the subject here, seen with does in a wooded landscape. it is deeply carved on a ruby flashed ground. This is an exceptionally large goblet; with the cover it measures an amazing 67cm/26³/₈ in.*

4

4 *A North Bohemian beaker, also with a canine subject, attributed to Egermann of Blottendorf. The green-tinted body is decorated in a gilded pattern, and the four raised medallions engraved with a hound and two stags are coloured to simulate semi-precious stones.*

5

6

LATE 19th CENTURY

1

2

1 *Stourbridge glass from c.1870-80 was made and decorated by a wide variety of techniques. The swirling-striped covered jar at left is inspired by Venetian glass. The ornate red-glass "cherry basket" has furnace-applied, colourless-glass feet and handles, while the egg-yolk-yellow jug bears a similarly applied colourless glass handle. The painted floral-decorated vase with crimped rim rests on opaline legs and is in imitation of white porcelain.*

2 *Late nineteenth-century Stourbridge cameo-cut glass primarily consisted of vases and other vessels with floral designs, like the two blue vases and the Japanese-inspired, pink orchid-decorated example at right. Rather more unusual is the portrait plaque at left and the red vase bearing a likeness of Queen Victoria.*

3

4

3 In the late Victorian period, Stevens & Williams, the Stourbridge glasshouse, produced colourful glass by traditional and innovative methods with a wide variety of decoration. The Silveria vase at left is in the asymmetrical, organic Art Nouveau mode, with silver foil sandwiched between two glass layers, whereas the crimped-rim vase with pull-up threading design beside it is more restrained and regular. The tall, double-gourd red vase has an exotic cameo-cut floral motif. Next to it is a startlingly modern-looking vase of so-called "moss agate" glass, a type in part developed by the young Frederick Carder (who later founded Steuben Glass). The pink goblet has been decorated with delicate criss-crossing white lines in the Venetian technique known as latticinio.

5

6

4 A soft, symmetrical leaf design covers the bulbous form of this vase by Stevens & Williams of Stourbridge, made c.1885. The white-glass vase is an example of dolce relievo, or soft relief glass, wherein a piece is flashed with a thin layer of coloured glass that is etched away to leave a design in low relief.

5 This cameo-glass vase, a classic form with gently fluted sides and applied handles, is decorated with the charming, fairy-tale-like subject of a child riding a grasshopper. Note the detailed, fairly high relief of the insect and figure, and the cloudier, flatter quality of the pool of water. It is American, and was made about 1880, possibly by the Boston & Sandwich Glass Co.

6 Jules Barbe liberally gilded this ornate glass loving cup, awash in Neoclassical motifs, around 1885. Its maker was Thomas Webb & Sons of Stourbridge.

117

LATE 19th CENTURY

1 Vaseline glass, so-called because of its resemblance to the murky yellowish ointment, was developed in the late nineteenth century and produced in the United States and Europe. Like many other pieces of Vaseline glass, this three-branched candlestick features applied decoration, specifically the knobs on the limbs.

2

2 The shimmering appearance of this bright green, late Victorian butter dish was effected by the inclusion of silver between the two layers of glass. The piece was made for Varnish & Co., London. The process involved either pouring the metal through a hole between the two layers before the final sealing, or covering the bottom layer with a coating of silver, then adding the top layer.

1

3 These three pieces of Stourbridge glass are examples of trailed and threaded glass of the late nineteenth century. Starting in the 1870s, much threading on glass was done by machine, which enabled the fine threads of coloured glass to encircle the entire body or rim of a vessel with exact precision and amazing speed.

4 These three American covered jars were made c.1885-95 by one firm, the Mount Washington Glass Works. The acorn and oak leaf-adorned jar on the left is of Albertine glass, the middle example is of Crown Milano gilded milk glass and the medallion-decorated piece at right is Royal Flemish glass.

3

4

6

5 English-born Joseph Locke created Amberina glass in the 1880s at the New England Glass Co. (it was patented in 1883). The red hue at the top of the Amberina bottle in this group was achieved by adding to the basic amber glass a tiny bit of gold that blazed red when reheated. The other two pieces are two-coloured variations on the same process.

6 Around the middle of the nineteenth century the Richardson glassworks of Stourbridge included a great deal of French-inspired opaline, or translucent-white, glass in their vast output. Those on either end have transfer-printed designs, while the toga-clad figures on the centre piece are hand painted.

5

REVIVALISM

2

1 Among the classic methods of Venetian glass decoration that attracted eager revivalists in nineteenth-century Britain was the latticinio *technique*, in which lacy white threads of glass are employed to create delicate internal designs resembling latticework of filigree. This English frilled-neck vase from the late 1800s is an elegant example.

2 Earlier Bohemian glass forms and types of decoration inspired late nineteenth-century European makers, as this trio of covered "*Historismus*", or historical-revival, vessels shows. At left is a goblet made c.1886 at the Ehrenfeld glassworks near Cologne; in the centre is a smoky-topaz Silesian goblet by Karl F.W.H. Siebenhaar, c.1870-79, and at right is a late nineteenth-century German copy of a humpen, or drinking glass.

1

3

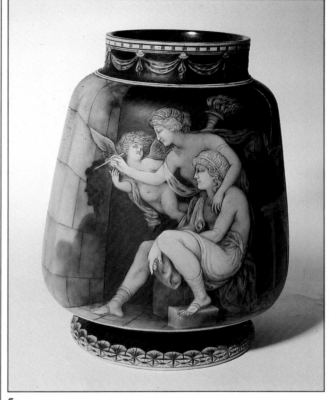

5

6

4

3 *A Venetian* millefiori *vase of the late nineteenth-century with an amber body internally decorated with elongated glass canes. The blurred appearance of the blossoms is quite different from the static, regular* millefiori *patterns on paperweights from France.*

4 *Anton Kothgasser, a painter at the Vienna porcelain factory, also applied the enamelling technique he used on china to glassware. This early nineteenth-century beaker in the Etruscan style is probably his design.*

5 *George Woodall, who was employed by Thomas Webb & Sons, created stunning cameo-cut vessels. This example, made c.1900, is called* The Origin of Painting.

6 *A large cameo with a Neoclassical theme embellishes this cut-glass pitcher from 1820. The complicated decorating technique, which was used in Bohemia, France and England, entailed embedding the cameos – in reality, white porcelain-like medallions known as sulphides – within the thick crystal glass.*

ENGLISH CAMEO

1 *Unlike the more ambitious, later cameo glass of Emile Gallé, Daum and other French glasshouses, with its multiple, multicoloured layers of glass, Stourbridge cameo glass generally consisted of a simple white relief motif against a dark ground. The outer layer was sometimes coloured, however, as on the yellow vase with pink-grape design (second from right) in this group of English cameo glass.*

2 *Background shades of blue predominate on these beautifully carved cameo-glass vessels, all of which – except for the unusual gilded fish in the foreground – sport floral designs. The ten pieces were made by Thomas Webb & Sons of Stourbridge, a glasshouse renowned for its cameo glass, which was produced under the skilled direction of the brothers George and Thomas Woodall.*

1

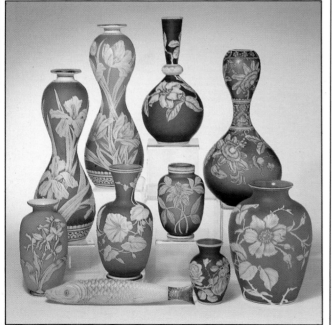

2

3

3 *Dating from around 1880, this cameo-glass vase by Thomas Webb & Sons features a skilfully carved, tellingly detailed floral and leaf design against an orange-glass ground. The brothers George and Thomas Woodall were in the main responsible for developing and expanding Webb's output of cameo-glass, whose background colours ranged from the palest yellow and pink shades to the deepest, darkest blues and reds.*

4

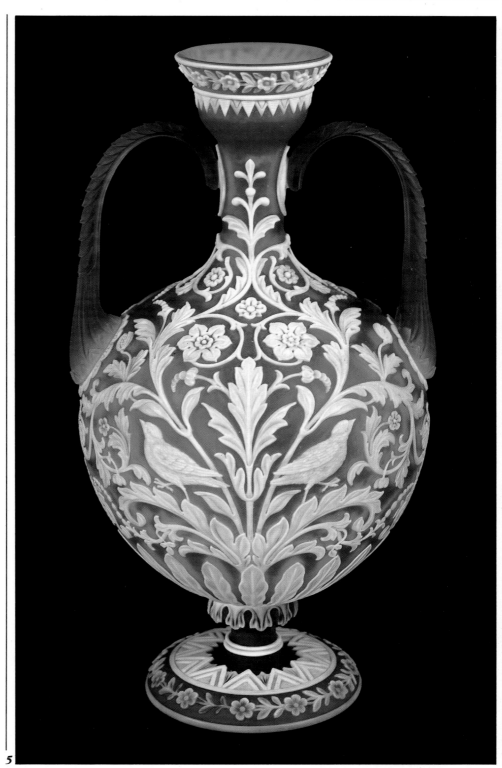

5

4 *A rich fruit and floral motif covers most of the surface of this carafe, to which a silvered metal handle, lid and spout are attached. Note the snakeskin-like texture of the blue ground, unusual in that most basal layers of coloured glass are flat, not carved.*

5 *The dense foliate and avian design on this Stourbridge cameo glass vase is nicely offset by a geometric zigzag motif on the foot and rim. The attached handles are not smooth but are carved with an organic design. The vase was made around 1884.*

PAPERWEIGHTS

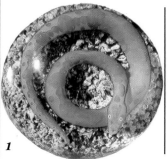

1 The great French glasshouse, Baccarat, was founded near Lunéville in 1765. By the mid-nineteenth century its fame was due largely to its paperweight production, these mostly of the millefiori (a thousand flowers) variety. The coiled green snake resting on glass pebbles that comprises this lampworked Baccarat paperweight is rare.

2 This fine and rare Baccarat "flat bouquet" weight includes the well-known Baccarat pansy in the bouquet of four flowers and a bud – a highly prized weight.

3 From top to bottom first column – top: St Louis "upright bouquet" weight; centre: Baccarat faceted sulphide weight with a profile head of Queen Victoria; bottom: St Louis concentric millefiori weight; second column – top: Small Baccarat "pansy" weight; below: Baccarat close millefiori weight; third column – top: Baccarat "scattered millefiori" weight; centre: Clichy swirl weight; bottom: St Louis concentric millefiori weight.

3

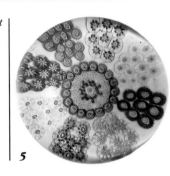

5 *An unusual Clichy paperweight with an overall design of a single large blossom. Its petals consist of clusters of eight different types of cut canes, while its pistil centre is made up of four additional varieties of colourful rods.*

5

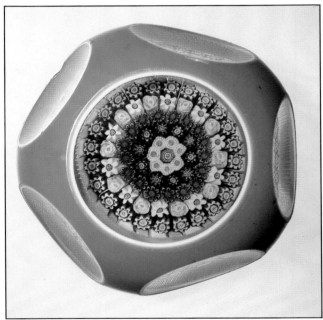

6

4 *All these weights are French, from the St Louis, Baccarat and Clichy factories, from the Clichy "swirl" to the rare Baccarat butterfly weights.*

6 *This Clichy "mushroom" weight is rare in having a double overlay of white and blue.*

4

PRESSED GLASS

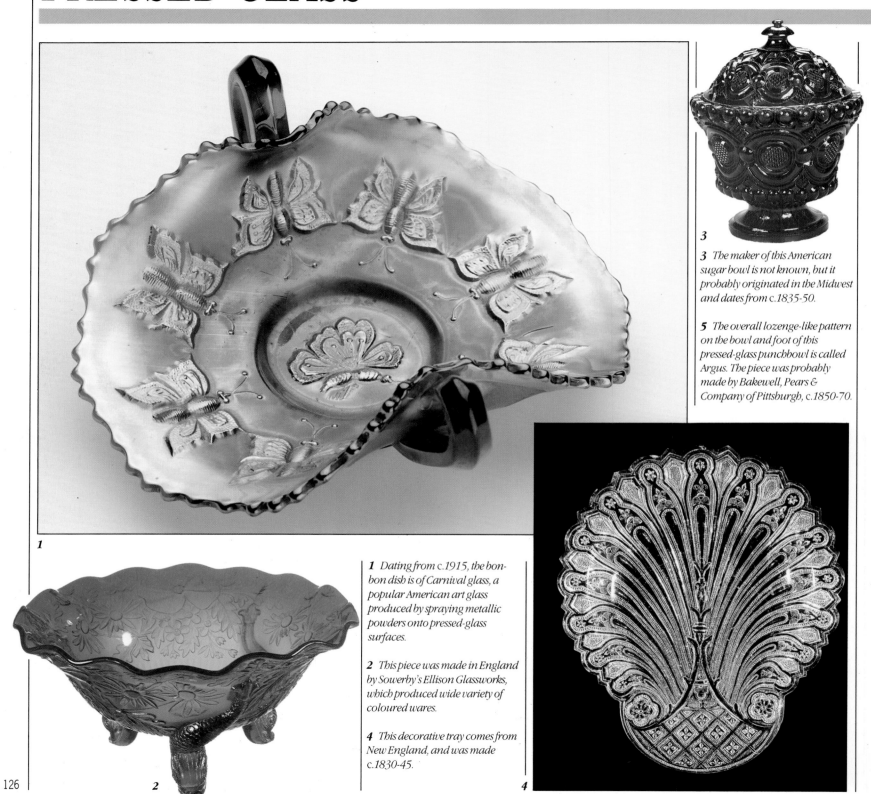

3 The maker of this American sugar bowl is not known, but it probably originated in the Midwest and dates from c.1835-50.

5 The overall lozenge-like pattern on the bowl and foot of this pressed-glass punchbowl is called Argus. The piece was probably made by Bakewell, Pears & Company of Pittsburgh, c.1850-70.

1 Dating from c.1915, the bonbon dish is of Carnival glass, a popular American art glass produced by spraying metallic powders onto pressed-glass surfaces.

2 This piece was made in England by Sowerby's Ellison Glassworks, which produced wide variety of coloured wares.

4 This decorative tray comes from New England, and was made c.1830-45.

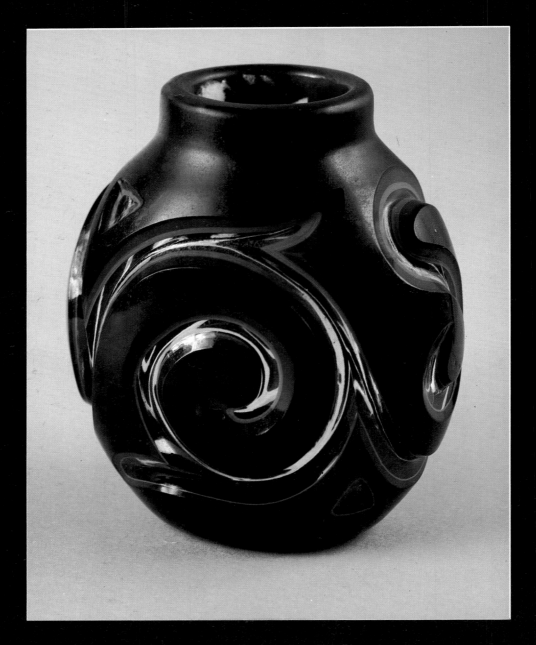

A rare intaglio-cut vase by Emile Gallé.

CHAPTER FIVE

THE ART NOUVEAU ERA

THE ART NOUVEAU ERA

Forget the snorting steam and piston stroke
Forget the spreading of the hideous town
Think rather of the pack horse on the down
And dream of London, small and white and clean
The clear Thames bordered by its gardens green.

The lines are from William Morris' *The Earthly Paradise*. But it was an intellectual dream – there was no going back except in imagination, and moreover, Morris' ideal of bringing art and "honest" designs to every man at an affordable price blinded him to the fact that to do this he would have to harness "the snorting steam and piston stroke". John Ruskin (1819-1900), who also detested machine-made ornament, and can be seen as the moving spirit of the Arts and Crafts movement, was equally impractical: his ideal of a "creative craftsman" took no account of the harsh realities of the working man's existence. However, both men were sincerely dedicated to the aim of "honest art and design" inspired by nature, and Morris' designs – which ranged from stained glass to metalwork, textiles and wallpaper – were extremely influential.

Although the Arts and Crafts movement did produce many attractive products, and several designers of talent and originality were associated with it, such as Christopher Dresser (1834-1904), whose simple and balanced style was influenced by Japanese art, it tended to become mere "arty-craftiness". Arthur Mackmurdo (1851-1942) followed the principles of Ruskin and Morris and founded his Century Guild in 1882, basing his designs on nature, as did Charles Rennie Mackintosh (1868-1928), also in Scotland, and the illustrator and designer Walter Crane (1845-1913)

Art Nouveau

The ideals of Morris and Ruskin, combined with the new interest in Oriental art and artefacts and the mysticism of the Pre-Raphaelites, provided the sources for the Art Nouveau style. Japanese art had been first introduced to Britain through the 1862 World Exhibition in London, and when it closed, exhibits were sold off by Farmers & Rogers of Regent Street in their "Oriental Warehouse". The manager of this emporium was Arthur Lasenby Liberty, whose own store Liberty & Co., also in Regent Street, was to become the main promoter of Art Nouveau in Britain. In France, in 1895, a shop called La Maison de l'Art Nouveau was opened in Paris by Samuel Bing, which gave the style its official name, though in Italy it was sometimes referred to as "Style Liberty".

The style was a short-lived one, which had died out by about 1910, but it caught on everywhere, and was much publicized by international exhibitions such as those in Paris in 1900 and St Louis and Turin in 1901. A number of

Emile Gallé created this engraved marqueterie-sur-verre *vase, in which the dense applied decoration on the neck and base are in stark contrast to the delicate underbody of the piece. One-off pieces such as this show the experimental, sculptural side of Gallé's technical virtuosity.*

art journals brought out at the turn of the century helped to make a wider public aware of it, as did advances in lithography, which brought the "New Style" to the streets, in the form of large advertising posters by artists such as Toulouse-Lautrec and Alphonse Mucha. The latter's posters for the great actress Sarah Bernhardt show women with the languid flower forms and crazily-scrolling hair so beloved of Art Nouveau, while the American dancer Loïe Fuller, who captivated Paris in 1891, became a living embodiment of it, dancing as "the lily", "fire", "night", "butterfly" and "bird". INTRODUCTION

The School of Nancy

Emile Gallé (1846-1904), whose name became synonymous with Art Nouveau, was born in Nancy, in France, and lived there all his life apart from a few years when he was a student. His father Charles owned a faience factory in St Clement, and Emile went into the family business about 1868, taking over as head in 1874.

Although a poet who believed that poetry could find expression through industry, Gallé was also a highly successful industrialist. His factory was well run, with about 300 employees at its peak, and he had his own retail outlets in both Paris and London. The designs were executed by Gallé and carried out by his work force.

Gallé's love of nature was his prime inspiration, and is constantly expressed in his designs, but after 1872, when he visited London and came into contact with the Aesthetic movement, Oriental influences can also be seen. The Impressionist painters had a great influence on him – he spent years trying to produce in glass the effects they obtained with paint on canvas.

He invented a bewildering number of different techniques, to which he gave poetic names, such as *verrière parlantes* (speaking glass), which was enamelled with medieval subjects inspired by illuminated manuscripts and inscribed with lines from poems. Many of his vases have quotations – from Mallarmé, Baudelaire, Poe, Maeterlinck, Victor Hugo, Gauthier, Alfred de Musset and his friend Robert de Montesquieu – and he saw the design of the vessel as visual expression of the words.

By the 1890s Galle had his own foundry and carpentry workshops, which made mounts in bronze, carved wood and wrought iron, which were an extension of the design of the vase or bowl. Silver mounts were sometimes executed by the greatest French silversmiths.

The Paris Exhibition of 1900 could be seen as a celebration of the electric light age, and lamps became an important part of Gallé's production from the late 1890s onwards. The earliest examples have a bronze base which held a cameo-glass shade, sometimes decorated with night scenes with flying bats inspired by a collection of poems by Montesquieu, *Les Chauve-Souris*. The largest group of lamps has a glass base and glass shade, usually acid-etched on two-, three- or even four-layered glass, which when illuminated gives a stunning effect. In the last few years before he died, Gallé designed some extraordinary lamps inspired by the mushroom, the most famous of which, *Les Coprins*, has three giant glass mushrooms set in a wrought-iron base.

Three years before his death, in 1901, Gallé and his friends Louis Majorelle (1859-1926) and Victor Prouvé

(1858-1943) founded the Alliance Provinciale des Artistes, which became known as the Ecole de Nancy. He had created a highly original style, which changed many of the old ideas as well as creating a great demand and encouraging a number of imitators.

A neighbour of Gallé's was Jean Daum, who acquired the Verrerie de Nancy in about 1875. He made mainly utilitarian glass, but when he died in 1885 his two sons, Auguste and Antonin (1864-1931), took over and in 1890 started producing "art glass" in the style of Gallé. Antonin Daum wrote in 1903 of their "study of living things, love of truth ... to poetic feeling in decoration, to logical principles of design and decoration". Gallé had begun by

This double-overlay table lamp also is one of Gallé's mushroom series, designed towards the end of his life. In keeping with the organic theme, it is decorated with a woodland scene on the stem – a place where the mushroom would naturally be found.

working in transparent glass decorated with enamels, and they did the same, but as the influence of Art Nouveau grew, they began to use "the language of flowers" and organic shapes. They exhibited at Chicago in 1893 and were awarded a Grand Prix at the Paris Exhibition in 1900. They produced acid-etched cameo designs on two- or three-colour grounds, while part or all of the rest of the vessel was given a "hammered metal" finish. They also produced a version of Gallé's marquetry technique.

Daum Frères also exhibited lamps at the Paris Exhibition in 1900. They made a range of floral lamps with flower-shaped shades, fitted to bronze stalks and bases made by Majorelle, who had been a schoolfriend of Antonin Daum and worked with him for many years.

Other French glassmakers

The Müller brothers, who came from a large family of glassworkers, were also influenced by Gallé, with whom they had trained before starting their own glassworks in 1860. They experimented constantly with decorative techniques, using hydrofluoric acid on multiple layers of coloured glass, to produce designs of landscapes with animals. They developed a technique called "fluogravure", in which the vessel, sometimes overlaid but usually of a single layer of glass, was painted with a pattern in intensely coloured enamels. After treatment in hydrofluoric acid, the enamel design stood out in "cameo" relief against the body of the vase. Metallic oxides were used in the enamel to give it an iridescent finish. Like Gallé and Daum Frères, they also produced an unusual range of lamps, in this case shaped as birds or animals.

Another artist working at this time was Eugène Rousseau (1827-91), who had also been a designer at the Sèvres porcelain factory. His designs were executed by the Clichy glassworks of Appert Frères. Rousseau had also fallen under the spell of Japanese art, and he designed cased-glass intaglio carved with views of Mount Fuji as well as simulated lacquer, "ice glass" and simulated rock crystal, shaped in bamboo forms. Although he had a workshop and retail shop, he did not produce glass on a commercial scale, and his work is now rare.

Tiffany glass

Louis Comfort Tiffany (1848-1933) was born into the rich and successful family of jewellers, Tiffany & Co. of New York. He originally studied painting, and travelled widely. While in the Middle East he became fascinated by the iridescence produced on ancient glass by centuries of burial and metallic oxides in the soil.

He became increasingly interested in the applied arts, and in 1879 founded an interior decorating company, under the name of Louis C. Tiffany & Co., and designed whole houses, down to the smallest detail, for such people

as Cornelius Vanderbilt, Lily Langtry and Mark Twain. In the course of this work he became interested in decorative glass windows, and engaged chemists to research new, brighter colours for the glass panes he required.

While continuing to run Louis C. Tiffany & Co., in 1885 he founded the Tiffany Glass Company. Essentially, he was the ruler of a business empire, but he knew how to surround himself with outstanding talent, and his wealth and artistic ability opened many doors to him. In 1889 he went to the Paris International Exhibition, where he met Bing, and the two men became friends and collaborators.

One of Tiffany's employees was an Englishman, Arthur Nash, who had worked at Webbs of Stourbridge, and was influential in the development of the iridescent glass that was later to be called Favrile (Nash had suggested the name Fabrile, an old English word for hand made or hand crafted). Iridescent glass was not a new discovery; other European firms had taken out patents, but Tiffany used it to exceptional advantage. He also understood how to market it, and the demand became considerable.

The output can be divided into two main categories, first, tableware produced in gold and sometimes blue iridescent glass, and second, display items made in a great variety of patterns, styles and techniques. The lustre-decorated wares included the well-known peacock-feather decoration.

Perhaps the best known of Tiffany productions are the lamps. Tiffany had known Thomas Edison, the inventor of the incandescent lamp, and had worked with him on light fittings for the new Lyceum Theatre in New York, the first one to be entirely lit by electricity. The standard-model lamps used the stained glass technique and had a bronze base supporting a leaded-glass shade, which provided an

Iridescent Art Nouveau glass in its many permutations is represented in this group of American and European vessels. The footed cup in the front and blue vase behind are by Tiffany, the large solid-hued Aurene vase in the front centre is by Steuben and the remaining pieces were produced by Loetz Witwe of Austria. The silver overlay on three of the Loetz pieces is especially lovely, providing strong floral motifs in relief against mottled iridescent backgrounds.

exotic and dim glow rather than a practical illumination.

Among the best-known designs are the Dragonfly Lamp, exhibited at the Paris Exhibition of 1900, the Wisteria Lamp of 1904, and many in the floral series such as laburnum, grape, apple blossom and so on. The Pond Lily Lamp, exhibited at Turin in 1902, won Tiffany a Grand Prix – it was a cluster of eighteen bronze stems issuing from a lily-pad topped by slender glass shades.

Austria

Tiffany glass is always marked, and no doubt one of the reasons for this was to prevent his many imitators from taking his markets. One of these was the Loetz-Witwe factory in Klostermühle, which was taken over by Johann Loetz' grandson Max von Spaun in 1879. Spaun introduced a vast range of different types of glass and took out patents for them. His glass in imitation of hardstones won a Grand Prix at the Paris International Exhibition of 1889, and in 1893 he exhibited several new types and colours at the Chicago World's Fair. He continued to research iridescence, and in 1899 introduced Papillon, which was flecked with raindrop shapes and made in many colours, followed by Actglas (clear and coral decoration) and Rusticana, with serpentine designs.

Loetz-Witwe also employed outside designers, including Koloman Moser, Josef Hoffmann, Otto Prutscher, Dagobert Peche and Michael Powolny (see Chapter Six). In 1903 Maria Kitschner, who had been a painter and studied in Prague, Munich and Paris, joined the firm, and remained there until 1914. She used a simplified form of straight functional lines with little decoration, usually on an iridescent gold or purple glass with no patterning.

In 1909, when Max von Spaun died, Adolf Beckert was appointed artistic director. He stayed only for two years, but in that time commissioned a wide range of tablewares in clear or frosted glass with enamel decoration. He also introduced a range of cameo glass.

The firm of Lobmeyr started as a retail business in Vienna in 1822. After expanding in both retail and manufacturing, Josef Lobmeyr bought a glassworks in Marienthal in 1837, took over a rival firm in 1838 and in 1851 became allied to one of the great Bohemian glassmaking families when his daughter Louise married Wilhelm Kralik, the owner of another glassworks, Meyr's Neffe. The company, J & L Lobmeyr, of which Ludwig Lobmeyr was sole director from 1864-1902, exhibited in Paris in 1878, and produced a vast range of fine-quality tableware and art glass, in crystal and coloured glass. Apart from this unexciting but stalwart production, they also commissioned designs from outside artists and used the talents of many of the best in Austria, such as Rudolf Marschall, Otto Tauschek, Antoinette Krasnik, Otto Prutscher and Josef Hoffmann.

Tiffany Studios' Wisteria Lamp has a simple bronze tree-trunk-like base and a glorious low-hanging shade made up of blue blossoms pendent from a web of bronze branches. It dates from around 1902. Wisteria featured on several Tiffany leaded-glass lamps, as well as on windows in his own Long Island, NY, home, Laurelton Hall (outside which wisteria actually bloomed in the spring).

INSPIRATIONS

Sinuous female figures with swirling draperies were the stock-in-trade of Art Nouveau, and pieces such as this biscuit-porcelain dancer (**1**) had a considerable influence on glassmakers, particularly Gallé and Lalique. This is one of a group of fifteen, designed as a table setting by Agathon Léonard, and was exhibited in 1900.

Some time before the peak of the movement, the naturalistic floral motifs in bright, clear colours seen on Persian ceramics (**2**) had become an inspiration to trend-setters such as William Morris and the great potter William de Morgan. Such themes quickly became incorporated into the repertoire of glassmakers.

1

2

The "new style" was disseminated through international exhibitions, art journals and, most important of all, posters, which brought it to a wide public. Alphonse Mucha (**4**), one of the major exponents, was poster designer to the actress Sarah Bernhardt for six years.

The American dancer Loïe Fuller captivated Paris in the 1890s, becoming a living embodiment of Art Nouveau. This gilt-bronze lamp (**5**) idealizes her in the best tradition of the time – more flower than woman.

3

William de Morgan also revived the lustre techniques seen on this Persian Savafid bottle (**3**), and similar effects were achieved in glass, notably by Louis Comfort Tiffany, whose iridescent glass became hugely successful.

MONACO·MONTE·CARLO

CHEMINS DE FER P.L.M.
Billets d'Aller & Retour_ Billets Circulaires
Billets d'Aller & Retour collectifs de famille à prix réduits.
TRAJET en 16 HEURES par TRAINS de LUXE

4

5

ARTS AND CRAFTS

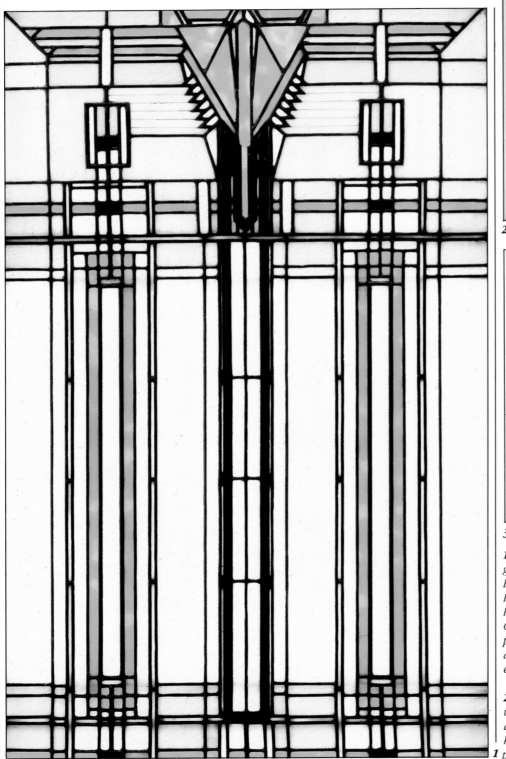

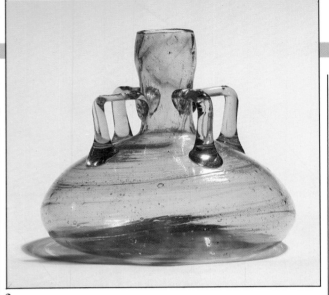

3

1 *Frank Lloyd Wright's leaded-glass skylight for the B. Harley Bradley House in Kankakee, Illinois, dates from 1900. The Prairie School architect's Arts and Crafts designs largely featured protomodern geometric motifs, and indeed this window could easily be mistaken for Art Deco.*

2 *Christopher Dresser applied his versatile design talent to glass, among other mediums. This four-handled sea-green bottle was produced by James Couper & Sons*

of Glasgow and is an example of the firm's Clutha glass, developed around 1885. Clutha is an Old Scottish word meaning cloudy.

3 *The designer of this elegant Clutha glass bowl is not known, but it was made by James Couper & Sons of Glasgow, c. 1885-1905. Note the handsome metal mount, of a typical organic design of the Arts and Crafts period.*

2

1

4

5

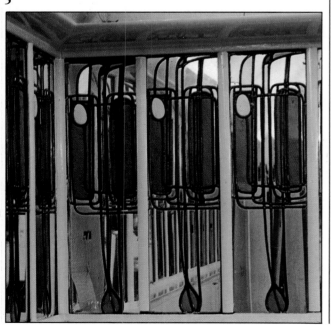

6

4 C.R. Ashbee's Guild of Handicraft created the lovely silver mount on this 1901 decanter. The green-glass body was made by James Powell & Sons of Whitefriars and designed by Ashbee himself.

5 Miss Cranston's Willow Tea Rooms, Glasgow, designed by Charles Rennie Mackintosh, featured a multitude of leaded-glass panels and doors. The semi-abstract, semi-organic motifs are typical of Mackintosh and the Glasgow School.

6 This delicate glass and silver centrepiece was made by the Whitefriars Glassworks of James Powell & Sons to Harry Powell's design in 1906. The feathery green streaks in the glass are echoed by the undulating silver wires of the mount.

IRIDESCENT

1 *The gilt-iridescent quartet of Tiffany pieces is largely indebted to ancient vessels for its forms. But for the trail of lozenges decorating the rim of the tall vase in the middle, the pieces are smoothly and solidly golden in hue.*

2 *Max Ritter von Spaun, longtime director (from 1879 to 1908) of Loetz Witwe in Klöstermuhle, designed these three iridescent vases for the Austrian firm c. 1898. The relief decoration on the example at right is especially lovely. It was handsome, innovative designs such as this that caused some to rate Loetz glass more highly than Tiffany's Favrile.* **2**

3

4

3 The wide range of Loetz iridescent glass, seen here in a group of thirteen, was highly impressive, from frilled-neck vases and vessels with silver overlay to examples with feathery or leafy internal trailings in diverse hues.

4 The glistening iridescence on the vessels of Louis Comfort Tiffany took a variety of guises. At left is a vase of Cypriot glass, with gilded "drippings" streaming down its mottled surface. On the middle vase, the abstract leaves set amid streaky tendrils are markedly different from the regular stylized pads on the dramatically rimmed example at right, which are neatly suspended on a ground of horizontal striations.

139

IRIDESCENT

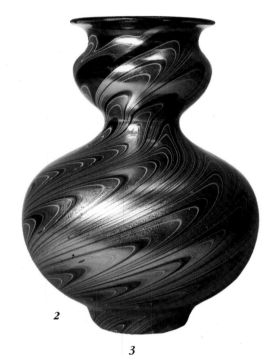

1

1 *This golden-green assortment of iridescent glass is attributed to Loetz Witwe, the Austrian glass-house whose products were the top European rivals to Tiffany's. The two shell-shaped vessels, with their stylized-wave bases, are especially attractive.*

2 *Dating from c. 1890, this double gourd-shaped, wide-necked Tiffany Favrile vase is decorated with a rich streaked and trailing iridescent design that resembles the marbleized pattern sometimes seen on the endpapers of old books.*

2

3

3 *A rich pulled-thread decoration of wavy lines covers this pair of Loetz iridescent-glass vases. The Austrian firm was founded in Bohemia in 1836 and at first produced stone, coloured and cameo glass. Its iridescent glass, however, made under Max Ritter von Spaun (grandson of the firm's founder, Johann Loetz), probably brought Loetz its greatest success.*

4 The smooth-surfaced paperweight-glass vase at left included iridescent streaking, whereas the Cypriot-glass vase at right has a rough, mottled texture with some iridescence. Both are by Louis Comfort Tiffany.

5 At one time in Europe Loetz glass surpassed that of Tiffany in popularity. With Max Ritter von Spaun at the firm's helm, Loetz produced an impressive output of shimmering vessels such as these; even their types of iridescence varied widely, from the splashed variety on the goosenecked example second from right to the feathery type on the bulbous-necked model in the centre.

FLORAL THEMES

1

1 This trio of French cameo glass features the ubiquitous floral motifs of Art Nouveau. All were produced in Nancy, the wheel-carved crocus vase at left by Daum Frères, the footed bowl in the middle by André Delatte and the lime-green vase at right by Emile Gallé. The Gallé vase comprises overlaid and etched glass, and its main carved-glass flowerheads, with amber centres, have been applied to the ground.

Galle

2 *Gallé's intense love of nature manifested itself in his furniture, glass and pottery creations. His vase at left depicts a moody, blue-dominated landscape, while that in the centre is a more detailed botanical study of individual clematis blossoms and leaves. The mould-blown and overlaid vase at right is faintly opalescent and features plum branches in low relief, their lush fruits in sculptural high relief.*

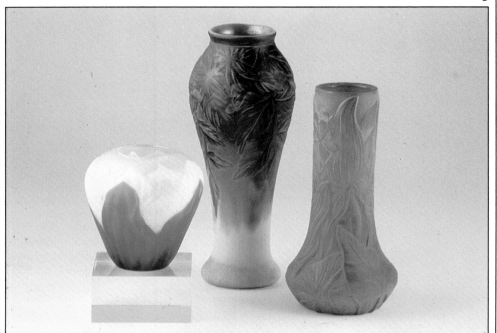

3 *The greatest proponent of nature-inspired Art Nouveau in the United States was Louis Comfort Tiffany, whose creations included furniture, pottery, metalwork and blown and stained glass. The Favrile glass vase at left depicts calla lily blossoms in a surround of rich green fronds. Unlike many of his French counterparts, notably Gallé, Tiffany was less concerned with truth to nature than with technique, texture and dramatic effect.*

FLORAL THEMES

1 *The Pond Lily floor lamp by Louis Comfort Tiffany (after 1902) comprises a bronze base of waterlily pads, a stand of twelve intertwining stems and, at the top, twelve Favrile glass blossoms. Similar glass shades could also be found on chandeliers and table lamps by the Art Nouveau master, whose oeuvre was dominated by floral motifs.*

2 *Emile Gallé, leading figure in the Ecole de Nancy, was both a keen observer of nature and a remarkable innovator in glass. This thick-walled vase from the 1890s has an otherworldly look, with its bright-hued leaves and blossoms seeming to float on an icy-white ground.*

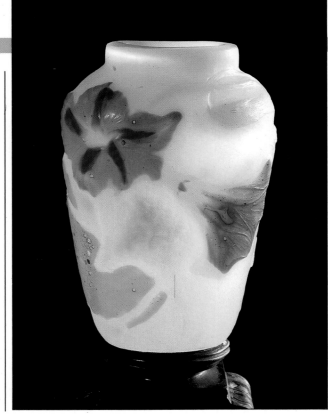

2

3

1

4

3 *As this assortment of Art Nouveau cameo-glass vessels clearly shows, flora in many forms – leafy, flowering, even bare and wintry – were a universal turn-of-the-century theme. The three examples at left are by Emile Gallé, as is the tall vase at right, while the blue, berry-bedecked vessel in the centre is by the Austrian glassmaker, Loetz. The distinctive signature of 'Daum Nancy' can be seen on the tall vase third from right; the same firm produced the small spherical vase with a wintry landscape to its left.*

4 *Like many of his outstanding lighting devices, Emile Gallé's Wisteria lamp, c. 1900, has a dome shade whose floral motif is repeated on its bulging cylindrical base. Both elements are of yellow glass overlaid with purple, blue and brown, and both contain the designer's appropriately florid script signature.*

5 *This pair of Gallé cameo-glass vases, c. 1900, is decorated with a floral motif in two shades of blue, achieved by cutting a double overlay of glass to reveal the pale lemon ground below.*

5

EMILE GALLE

1 Many of Gallé's early enamelled-glass vases were influenced by Oriental art. The swimming carp on this vase is decidedly Japanese in inspiration, as is the detailed – and fantastic – aquatic setting in which it swims.

2 An applied- and engraved-glass vase by Gallé, entitled Le Premier Gel d'Automne (the first frost of autumn), dating from c. 1903. The elaborate irregular rim is typical of many of Gallé's more symbolic pieces, which he often gave poetic names. Sometimes he even included appropriate verses on their surfaces.

5 *The Middle Ages provided the inspiration for this cylindrical, trefoil-rim vase dating from 1884-1900. Gallé called the pieces that featured words verrerie parlante (speaking glass), and here the vessel is inscribed in medieval-style script with La Ballade des Dames du Temps Jadis, after a poem by François Villon (b. 1431).*

6 *The unusual twisted-floriate handles of this Gallé vase have their motif echoed on the piece's base. The landscape panels are pure Japonisme, with their sketchy brush strokes and romantic Japanesque scenes.*

3

4

3 *The techniques and motifs of medieval glass also served as inspiraton to Gallé in the late nineteenth century. The enamelled, medieval-style decanter and liqueur set with tray dates from 1889.*

4 *Like Tiffany in America, Gallé looked to ancient Middle Eastern sources for the subjects and shapes of his glass. This two-handled bottle shows extensive use of decorative enamelled motifs borrowed from Syrian art.*

5

6

SHAPES

1

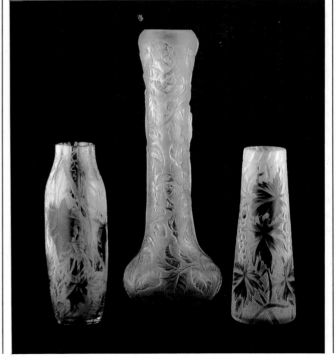

2

3

1 This stunning triple-overlay vase by Emile Gallé is additionally decorated with applied-glass elements. It features an underwater scene, complete with undulating, engraved waves all round. Its neck is somewhat unusual, and also seems to be applied as well. The muted green and mottled glass is appropriate for a subaquatic theme.

2 The double-gourd form of this blown and polished Gallé vase is rather unusual, as is the single applied "handle" of uncoloured glass which clings to and encircles the upper section of the piece like a branch.

3 This trio of elongated vases by Tiffany features leafy intaglio-cut designs. Though the forms are all basically cylindrical, the tapering neck of the vase at left, the bulbous bottom of the centre example and the nicely S-fluted neck of the piece at right – as well as the rich textures of all three vases – make their simple shapes secondary to their rich patterning.

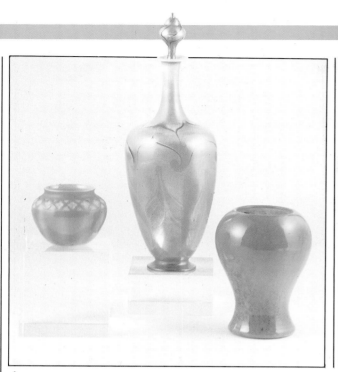

4

5

6

Gallé

4 *Tiffany was heavily influenced by both the forms and techniques used in ancient glass, both Eastern and Western. The marbleized paperweight-glass decanter in the middle is notably exotic. A lattice-work cameo-glass vase is at left, a lustre-glass vase at right.*

5 *Among Gallé's masterworks are his one-off glass creations, whose applied elements, unusual forms and often poetic titles make them stand out in his impressive oeuvre. This example is called* Feuille de chou *("Cabbbage Leaf"), and its undulating rim, applied veins of white glass and streaking throughout give it a unique partly abstract, partly organic appearance.*

6 *But for the pinched rim on the narrow-necked vase at left, the forms of these tall cameo-glass vases by Gallé are typical, regular and classic. Standard Gallé features also are the floral subjects depicted, with an additional one drawn from fauna – a dragonfly, another pet Gallé subject – on the example second from left.*

TECHNIQUES

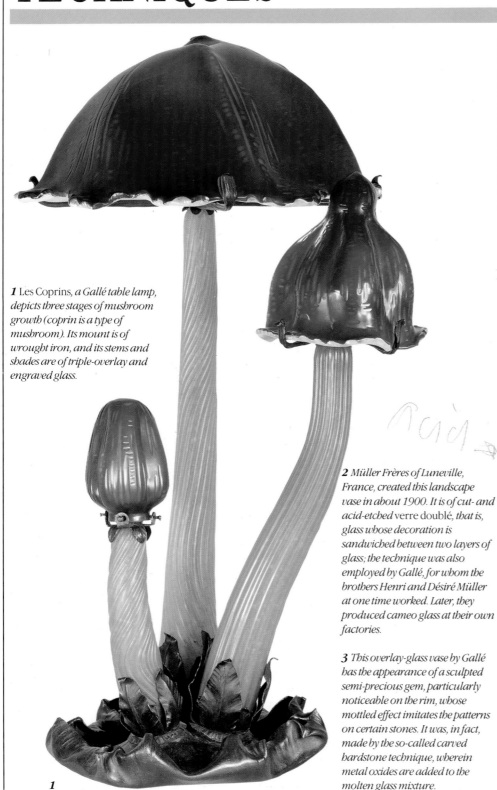

1 Les Coprins, *a Gallé table lamp, depicts three stages of mushroom growth (coprin is a type of mushroom). Its mount is of wrought iron, and its stems and shades are of triple-overlay and engraved glass.*

2 Müller Frères of Luneville, France, created this landscape vase in about 1900. It is of cut- and acid-etched verre doublé, *that is, glass whose decoration is sandwiched between two layers of glass; the technique was also employed by Gallé, for whom the brothers Henri and Désiré Müller at one time worked. Later, they produced cameo glass at their own factories.*

3 This overlay-glass vase by Gallé has the appearance of a sculpted semi-precious gem, particularly noticeable on the rim, whose mottled effect imitates the patterns on certain stones. It was, in fact, made by the so-called carved hardstone technique, wherein metal oxides are added to the molten glass mixture.

4 *The rich decoration on this oviform Tiffany Favrile glass vase from 1905 was achieved by both internal and external means. The mottled golden-hued lily pads are suspended inside the clear glass, whereas the frosted flower, reed and lily-pad motifs are engraved on the outside of the vase.*

5 *This unusual glass vase by Daum Frères of Nancy has a layer of black enamel etched with a gold thistle design. The double cross motif, seen at right, is the Croix de Lorraine, an elaborate example of the motif with which the brothers signed their pieces.*

6 *Antonin and Auguste Daum of Nancy created these two pinched-rim, rectangular-section bowls around 1900-06. Their mottled, mostly white bodies are decorated with floral motifs that have been hand-painted with enamel as well as acid-etched.*

4

5

6

TECHNIQUES

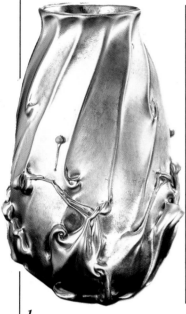

1 *The English-born Frederick Carder, who founded Steuben Glass in Corning, New York, in 1903, experimented with a variety of complex techniques. The iridescence on this blown Aurene vase – Carder's answer to Tiffany's Favrile glass – is extremely dense, and the swirled ribbing design is quite unusual, as is the quasi-abstract, irregular-patterned relief decoration towards the bottom.*

2 *This trio of Tiffany vases is made of paperweight glass, which means that the decoration has been applied on the inner glass shape and then encased in an outer layer. The resultant effect is lustrous and fluid, and the thick walls give the works a weighty substance.*

3 *A variety of decorative techniques was employed by the French Art Nouveau glass-makers – notably Gallé, Müller Frères and Daum Frères, whose busy factories produced these eleven vessels roughly at the turn of the century. The group shows examples of overlay, enamelled and acid-etched cameo glass, in diverse colours and shapes, but all featuring themes from nature.*

4

4 *Like his contemporaries in France, Louis Comfort Tiffany used a variety of techniques for his Art Nouveau glass, some traditional and others innovative. He marketed his glass wares under the name 'Favrile', a word derived from the Old English fabrile, or hand made. Unlike iridescent pieces, these three vessels feature subtle, matt, nature-inspired decoration.*

5 *The earthy tones of these two Daum Frères cameo vases give them a silhouette-like appearance. Their decoration – an autumnal landscape on the vase, left, and foxglove blossoms on the taller vase, right – has been wheel carved.*

5

STAINED GLASS

1 It was Tiffany's desire to translate the beauty of nature into "the speech of stained glass" and, beginning with experiments in the medium in 1872, he proceeded to develop a rich new artistic language. In this leaded-glass skylight, he deftly put together the pieces of his puzzle, from the minute mottled glass petals to the large elements of blue sky, to create a unique vision of nature.

2 The painter Edward Burne-Jones provided the design for this Morris & Co. stained-glass panel showing an allegorical figure of Justice standing within a typical leaf-strewn Arts and Crafts setting. Morris & Co., which was founded in 1874, concentrated on stained-glass windows during its early years, with William Morris designing over 150 windows himself and creating the decorative backgrounds of countless others.

3 *Tiffany Studios created this leaded-glass window, aglow with trumpet vine. Many Tiffany windows included elements – like the wooden trellis on this example – that in fact mimicked the panes of a normal window. Note the signature in the lower left-hand corner.*

4 *The proud peacock was a common motif in both the Arts and Crafts and Art Nouveau repertoires. In addition to decorating many of his Favrile glass vases with stylized peacock feathers, Tiffany fashioned the bird itself in leaded glass, its plumes a rainbow of hues. The window dates from 1890-1900.*

4

3

LAMPS

1 *This superb Dragonfly Lamp produced by the Tiffany Studios not only sports a stunning insect-embellished shade, but its base is equally impressive, being made of bronze "turtleback" iridescent glass tiles and tiny mosaic bits. Most Tiffany lamp bases were of patinated bronze alone, so even when it was produced it would have been a costly item.*

2 *Lamps became an important part of Gallé's production from the late 1890s, and several, like this leaded-glass, bronze and mosaic-tiled lamp, were decorated with night scenes of flying bats. These nocturnal creatures appeared in the work of other well-known Art Nouveau designers, such as René Lalique, who used the motif for some of his jewellery.*

2

3

4

3 *Emile Gallé often created lamps with both glass bases and shades, but he also collaborated with metalmaking firms, which in turn produced separate bases for his glass tops. The elaborate gilt-bronze base of this lamp is by one Emile Guillaume.*

4 *Although it has a simple tree-trunk patinated-bronze base, the richly florid shade of this Tiffany Studios lamp gives it a strong, showy appearance, appropriate for a lamp whose subject is roses.*

5 *The Austrian glassmaker Loetz created this handsome lamp, whose spherical iridescent-glass shade surmounts a gilt-metal base that is typical of Jugendstil, the Austrian Art Nouveau style. The opalescent glass cabochons set into the bottom of the base are amazingly like opals.*

5

Glass form in white and clear glass with fumed trailing. Sam Herman, 1970.

CHAPTER · SIX
THE 20th CENTURY

THE 20th CENTURY

With the great upheaval of the First World War, life changed dramatically, and so did art. The invention of the internal combustion engine brought the motor car, quickly followed by the submarine and the aeroplane, and new needs began to be met, in both architecture and the applied arts, by new materials and production techniques.

The dreamy, convoluted shapes of Art Nouveau went out of fashion, giving way to the Art Deco style, influenced by the geometric relationships of Cubist paintings, and to Modernism, in which function was held as the guiding principle that determined form. To a large extent, these two overlapped, but the Art Deco style was largely a French one, taking its name from the Exposition Internationale des Arts Décoratifs et Industriels Modernes, held in Paris in 1925. In architecture, which influenced all the applied arts, the chief exponents of Modernism were Le Corbusier in France, Walter Gropius and the Bauhaus in Germany, and Hendrik Berlage in Holland, and the effect of their ideas on glass as well as the other applied arts was seen at the 1925 Exposition.

France: the studio glassmakers

Not all artists were devoted to the Bauhaus ideal of well designed objects capable of machine production, and a new distinction between industrially produced luxury objects and the studio productions of individual artists began to emerge. This is typified, in the field of glass, by the factory productions of René Lalique (1860-1945) on the one hand and the "one-off" pieces of Maurice Marinot (1882-1960) on the other.

Marinot, born at Troyes in France, started as a painter, studied at the Ecole des Beaux Arts in Paris, and exhibited at the Salon d'Automne and Salon des Indépendants between 1905 and 1914. In 1911 he visited the small glassworks of the Viard brothers at Bar-sur-Seine and, entranced by the beauty of glass, began designing it for the Viards, in simple shapes, painted with decorations of figures and flowers in rich enamel colours.

But Marinot wanted to "work" the glass himself, and taught himself the technique, working at the furnace alone or with just a boy to help him. He went on to explore the colour and texture of the material to develop a unique style – heavy-walled bottles and jars with simple outlines and coloured effects between inner and outer layers – for which he became well known. Numerous articles were written on his work, and his exhibits at the 1925 Exposition were widely acclaimed.

He naturally had followers, the most distinguished of whom being Henri Navarre (1885-1970), André Thuret (1898-1965) and Georges Dumoulin (b 1882). Navarre, a sculptor, also worked with thick-walled glass, with internal decoration of swirls and whorls of sombre colour, and

André Delatte's vase of red glass, with its frieze of dancers against a stylized-floral blue band, is a blaze of Art Deco, a style whose bright colours and exotic aspects were in part influenced by Diaghilev's Ballets Russes, which may in fact have directly inspired the motif on this piece.

in addition he made a series of sculptures of human faces, mostly in clear crystal.

Thuret produced internal swirls of colour, using tools to pinch the glass into undulating shapes, while Dumoulin, who had worked at the Sèvres porcelain factory, made in the late 1920s a series of stoppered bottles and vases with internal colour and bubble effects, often applied on the exterior with spiral decoration.

Aristide Colotte, originally an engraver, worked with

large and heavy blocks of crystal glass. These were carved, and both acid and cutting and grinding tools were used to achieve a pure transparency. Jean Sala, the son of a Spanish glassmaker, used a lightweight metal full of bubbles and imperfections. He and his father made a collection of glass fish for the aquarium in Monaco.

Pâte de verre

This is a material made of finely crushed pieces of glass mixed with a medium. It was a process known in ancient Egypt, but lost, and rediscovered in 1885 by Henri Cros, who had experimented with it when he worked at the Sèvres porcelain factory. In 1906 Daum Frères had started a *pâte de verre* workshop headed by Alméric Walter (1859-1942), who had also been at Sèvres. They made small statuettes, small animal sculptures, vases and bowls encrusted with lizards, frogs, newts and crabs reminiscent of the late sixteenth-century pottery of Bernard Palissy. The dancer Loïe Fuller inspired two models, as she had done in Sèvres porcelain. Walter worked with H. Berge at

The ancient Egyptian technique of making pâte-de-verre *glass, which involves mixing finely crushed glass with an adhesive medium and heating it in a mould, was revived in the late 1800s by Frenchman Henri Cros. Fine pâte de verre in both the Art Nouveau and Art Deco styles appeared throughout the early years of the twentieth century. The blue vase and bird-topped box here are by Gabriel Argy-Rousseau, the thistle-decorated tray and Neoclassical figure by Alméric Walter.*

Daum, and pieces made by them are signed with both names.

François Emile Décorchement (1880-1971) also worked in this technique, specializing in simple shapes and the minimum of decoration. In 1921 Gabriel Argy-Rousseau (1885-1953) started a firm called Les Pâtes-de-Verre d'Argy-Rousseau, and produced a wide range of decorative wares in a very clear version of the material called *pâte-de-cristal*. He made a wide range of shapes, vases, pots, lamps, pendants, ashtrays and bowls, sometimes in shades of rich purple and mauve. In addition to plant and animal subjects he also used abstract designs.

René Lalique

Lalique (1860-1945) had been a famous designer of luxury jewellery in the Art Nouveau style, but became increasingly interested in glass, and gradually moved from designing and making jewels for a wealthy but small clientèle to manufacturing well-designed glass for a much wider public, founding a new glasshouse in 1918. He produced a variety of shapes in a colourless glass with a frosted surface, often moulded with female figures, birds, fish and flowers in controlled patterns. He also used abstract designs.

In 1920 he was given orders for extravagant light fittings for the luxury liner *Paris*, followed by similar commissions for the *Ile de France* in 1927 and the *Normandie* in 1930. The range of his production was enormous, and at the 1925 Exposition he had his own pavilion. In addition to making very stylish tableware, he was very much a "man of the moment", designing car mascots as well as lamps, illuminated decorative panels, clock cases, wall panels, tables, glass jewellery and figures, such as the famous *Susanna at her bath*.

Lalique died in 1945 at the age of eighty-five, having created a new style and become internationally famous. His son took over the firm. It was inevitable that he should have his copyists, and the firms of Etling, d'Avisn, Genet & Michon and Sabino all produced glass in the manner of Lalique. It was even copied in Bohemia and England – surely a case of "imitation being the sincerest form of flattery".

Scandinavia and Holland

In Sweden the Society of Industrial Design (Svenska Slojdforeningen) set out to apply good design to mass-produced articles, and Modernism, with its stress on function, seemed to provide the answer. Many Swedish factories took on artists to design their production, among them being the glassworks at Orrefors, which appointed Simon Gate (1883-1945) and Edward Hald (1883-1980) in 1916 and 1917 respectively.

Both had trained as artists, and both had everything to learn about practical glassmaking. Initially, the idea was to

Above Largely due to the Murano firm of Venini, traditional techniques of Italian glassmaking were revived in the mid-twentieth century, and innovative methods introduced. The two-coloured vase at left is attributed to Ferro Lazzarini, the centre vase is by Salviati and the clear vase at right is by Venini.

Below Edvard Hald created this bowl for the Swedish firm Orrefors. Dating from 1917-20, it is made of Graal glass, a refinement of cameo glass.

improve on the Gallé-style cased glass the factory already produced, and they developed two techniques called Graal and Ariel. The former was a modification of the cameo technique, with a final clear casing which gave the glass a fluid appearance, while Ariel had a pattern sandblasted onto the body and a second casing of clear glass over it.

But it was their engraved glass which was destined to win fame, both in Stockholm and abroad. Gate designed heavy vessels with deep engraving, while Hald preferred shallow engraving with designs that were obviously influenced by his former painting teacher Matisse. After 1930 both Gate and Hald were much influenced by Marinot's simple shapes.

Two other Orrefors artists of note are Vicke Lindstrand (b 1904), working there from 1928 to 1941, and the sculptor Edvin Ohrstrom, who was on the permanent staff from 1936. Deep relief engraving in a simple style on a heavier glass became popular, and an outstanding example is Lindstrand's *Shark-killer* vase, designed in 1937.

Orrefors is still the centre of the industry in Sweden. Many artists have continued to develop the Ariel and Graal techniques, and Sven Palmquist (b 1906), at Orrefors since 1936, invented Ravenna glass, which has a mosaic-like appearance using brightly coloured inlaid patterns. It has been called one of the finest creations of modern glass. Lindstrand, who became head designer at Kosta in 1950, had an enormous output and used all the Orrefors techniques of Graal, Ariel, cutting and engraving.

At the Holmegaard glassworks in Denmark the architect Jacob Bang was appointed as designer in 1925, and the factory produced tablewares and decorative vases with simple engraved linear designs, also influenced by Marinot. In Norway, at the Hadelands glassworks, Sverre Pettersen designed some beautiful tableware and vases

from 1928 – often as special orders for individual customers. During the 1930s Pettersen experimented with sandblasted decoration, and from 1937 onwards the sculptor Svale Kyllingstad designed engraved vases for Hadeland.

After the Second World War Hadelands enlarged its output of art glass, introducing colour, and Willy Johansson and Herman Bongard (both b 1921) were taken on as designers in 1947. Johansson used inlaid colours and textural effects, and produced a very interesting ruby-red glass which changes to sea-green at the base of the vessel. Arne Jon Jutrem (b 1929), who worked for Hadeland from 1950, used simple robust shapes, sometimes with engraved and sandblasted abstract patterns.

The glass factory at Riikimäki in Finland produced engraved glass very much in the Orrefors style from 1928, but in 1938 the architect Alvar Aalto designed a series of vases in clear coloured glass for the factory at Karhula-Iittala which were more individual. Their asymmetric forms and undulating lines were reminiscent of the bentwood furniture he also designed at the time.

Slightly later, the designer Gunnel Nyman (1909-48), although she died at the early age of thirty-nine, brought Finnish glass to international notice. She started as a furniture designer, but by the early 1940s had evolved a very personal and poetic style in glass. Her "folded models" show a great sympathy for the pliability of the material. She worked in transparent glass with symmetric-

The Monart glass range, produced in the 1920s and '30s by John Moncrieff Ltd in Perth, Scotland, comprised thick-walled vessels whose internal decoration – streaks, bubbles and the like – were British variations on the one-off creations of Maurice Marinot in Paris.

al patterns of tiny bubbles, sometimes combined with cutting used in original ways.

The two other outstanding Finnish designers of this time are Tapio Wirkkala (b 1915) and Timo Sarpaneva (b 1926), working for Karhula-Iittala, the former since 1947 and the latter since 1950. Wirkkala used simple engraved lines to emphasize form, and also evolved a technique of blowing glass into wooden moulds from which it takes the texture of the wood. In 1954 Sarpaneva exhibited some flower vases which were really abstract sculpture at the Milan Triennale.

During the nineteenth century the Leerdam glassworks in Holland, founded in 1765, had produced utilitarian glassware, but after the appointment of P. M. Cochius as director just before the First World War, the factory commissioned designs from well-known architects like Berlage (1856-1934), Karel de Bazel (1869-1923) and Frank Lloyd Wright (1869-1959). In 1922 Chris Lebeau (1878-1945), a painter and industrial designer, joined Leerdam, and helped to found the Unica Studio which produced "one off" items by various designers.

He was succeeded as principal designer in 1923 by Andries Dirk Copier (b 1901), who had been with the factory in 1917 and became a very innovative designer, winning a First Prize at the Paris Exposition in 1925. He was artistic director for over fifty years, designing both quality table glass and collectors "art glass". In addition to the unique Unica series of vases, he also started Serica, a

by the finest engravers of the area, which had a long history of glassmaking. From 1920-1937 Marianne Rath (b 1904) worked as a designer, and in 1925 Jaroslav Horejc engraved superbly in *hochschnitt* (high relief) technique.

Germany produced one of the finest glass engravers of the twentieth century in Wilhelm von Eiff (1890-1943), who had learned engraving on both glass and metal at an early age. He travelled around Europe, working for a time at Lalique's jewellers' studio and with the glass engraver Charles Michel in Paris. He was influenced by the teaching of the Munich designer Bernhard Pankok at the School in Stuttgart, and in 1922 himself became professor in cutting and engraving on glass and precious stones at the same school.

His very fine *hochschnitt* engraving shows a consummate mastery of the art, and because he was both designer and executor his work has great force and originality. He ranged from Classical styles to bold Modernist designs, and also did intricately detailed miniature portraits in both glass and gemstones with great finesse.

Von Eiff's teaching was highly influential, and his students came from all over the world. Helen Monro Turner, who founded the Juniper Workshop in Scotland in 1956, trained under him, as did the Japanese Kizo Kagami, who now has his own factory, the Kagami Crystal Works.

Other pupils continue the German tradition of fine engraving, for example Konrad Habermeier (b 1907), who designed for Gralglashutte very restrained patterns on the simplest of shapes. Three others worked as freelance engravers – Hans Model from 1943, Marianne Schoder from 1938 and Nora Ortlieb from 1943.

Italy

After the First World War a truly modern style was created in Italy by two men, Paolo Venini (1895-1959) and Ercole Barovier (b 1889). Venini trained for the law although he came from a family of glassblowers, and started a law practice in Milan before realizing his true interest. He then went into partnership with a young Venetian, Giacomo Cappellin (b.1887) who had a gift shop in Milan, and they purchased a Muranese glassworks in 1924.

They made copies of the kind of glasses seen in eighteenth-century Venetian paintings, which in their simplicity were a startling contrast to the over-elaborate Venetian style of the time. They exhibited at the 1925 Paris Exposition, but the partnership split up in the same year, and Venini set up his own factory, Venini & C, in Murano.

He continued to make simple vessels, but he started to use colour, as well as the old-established techniques of *millefiori* and *vetro a filigrano*. He also experimented with textures, producing between 1928 and 1934 such effects as *vetro pugeloso*, an opaque glass with small air bubbles; *vetro corroso* (corroded glass), treated with

limited-edition series of vases. His designs were elegant but simple, some being in thin glass and others thick-walled, with internal bubbles and seaweed effect. In 1928 he designed "perfect sphere" vases which were copied all over the world.

Austria and Germany

The Wiener Werkstatte, founded in 1903 as an association of workshops, gave artists and craftsmen in various media an opportunity to work side by side. Joseph Hoffmann (1870-1956), who had studied architecture and designed one of the rooms at the first Vienna Secession exhibition, was co-founder with Koloman Moser (1868-1918), and designers included Michael Powolny (1871-1954), who taught at the Vienna School of Arts and Crafts from 1909 till 1941, and Dagobert Peche (1887-1923), who was a member from 1917 until his death. Powolny's designs for glass are usually of simple form, enamelled with abstract friezes and panels, and Peche used enamelled figures and flowers.

In 1918 Stephan Rath, who was a nephew of Ludwig Lobmeyr, founded a branch of the main firm in Steinschonau under the name of J. & L. Lobmeyr Neffe Stephan Rath. Rath designed the glass himself, and it was decorated

In 1921 the German metal factory Württembergische Metallwarenfabrik (WMF) set up a glass studio under the direction of the Austrian Wilhelm von Eiff. Their Ikora range of heavy, often bubbled-glass, created around 1925, was similar to the output of Marinot, Schneider, Moncrieff and others. This vase, designed by Karl Wiedmann, is probably an example of Ikora glass made c.1935.

chemicals; and *vetro sommerso* (underwater glass), which was coloured glass with air bubbles encased in an outer layer of clear glass.

These were followed in the 1940s by *vetro tessuto* (woven glass), to the design of Carlo Scarpa, and *vetro pezzato* (patchwork glass), which had a fascinating effect of different-coloured canes moulded together. In the 1950s and '60s Venini produced the famous *Morandi Bottles* inspired by the painter Morandi. In 1976 Venini's grand-daughter Laura de Santillana worked for the firm, and her free-cast glass plate with mosaic canes called *Numeri* won an award at the 1979 Corning Exhibition.

Ercole Barovier came from a very old Muranese glassmaking family and was artistic director of the firm Barovier & Toso. His shapes, too, are simple, but with a gently flowing line, and during the 1920s he also experimented with texture and colour, producing in 1927 his *Primavera* glass, with a mottled surface. In 1940 came *rugiada* glass, giving the effect of fine dewdrops on the surface, and *vetro gemmato*, simulating natural stone.

Britain and America

The world-wide success of British cut crystal largely discouraged any attempt to experiment with new techniques in the twentieth century, but there was one important exception – the Whitefriars factory in London under the directorship of James Hogan (1883-1948). Fine designs for simple blown glass were produced by Barnaby Powell (1891-1939), who was the last member of the Powell family of the Whitefriars factory, and by William J. Wilson, who was a co-director with Hogan.

The young New Zealand architect Keith Murray (1892-1981) had become interested in glass after a visit to the 1925 Exposition. In 1932 some of his designs were produced by Whitefriars, and in the same year he arranged to work as a designer for the firm of Stevens & Williams in Stourbridge for three months of the year. He produced simple forms, mostly undecorated, for tableware, and some vessels which had flat-cut faceting or well-controlled engraved designs. One series of vases was engraved with cacti, which was a popular plant in the 1930s.

Amazingly, the only other designer working on British glass at this time was Clyne Farquharson, a professional glass designer who created some elegant vases with cut and engraved patterns for the firm of John Walsh in Birmingham. There was an attempt to revitalize design in preparation for the British Art in Industry exhibition in London in 1935, and artists such as Paul Nash, Graham Sutherland, Eric Ravilious and Dame Laura Knight were commissioned to design glass for Stuart & Sons of Stourbridge. But these artists had a very limited knowledge of the actual making of glass, and inevitably it

showed in their work. The firm of J. Moncrieff in Perth, Scotland, produced their Monart glass between the wars – this had swirls of internal colouring and bubbles and showed some affinity with art glass of the Continent.

The Depression cast a terrible shadow over industrial production in America in the 1930s. Tiffany died in 1933, and the Tiffany Studios went bankrupt; the firms of Quezal and Handel & Co. closed down in 1925 and 1936 respectively. It was the end of an era.

The only surviving hope was the Steuben factory at Corning in New York State. It had been founded in 1903 by an Englishman, Frederick Carder (1863-1963), and was named after a hero of the American War of Independence, Baron von Steuben. In 1918 it was incorporated into the vast Corning Glass Works, and in 1933 Carder, who had created a line of coloured glass, was replaced as head of the firm, and it was restyled Steuben Glass Inc. A young architect, John Monteith Gates, was the chief director, and the sculptor Sydney Waugh was appointed as designer.

Their new high-grade crystal glass was fashioned into simple blown forms with fine engraving. Waugh's *Gazelle Vase* of 1935 shows the influence of Hald's style of engraving at Orrefors. In 1940 Gates commissioned designs from a number of prominent artists including Henri Matisse, Marie Laurencin, Eric Gill and Jean Cocteau. He had a genius for marketing and instigated exclusive shops within leading stores – a man well ahead of his time.

The American glassmaker Steven Newell created this cased and sandblasted vase at The Glasshouse in London around 1981. Its somewhat disturbing subject matter is two profiles, purple (glass) in the face, forever frozen in angry confrontation.

INSPIRATIONS

Divinité Solaire (**1**) by Gustave Milos, a Hungarian-born painter and sculptor who worked in a variety of media including copper and plaster. The Cubist aesthetic was a permeating influence on the fine and applied arts from the 1920s onwards.

1

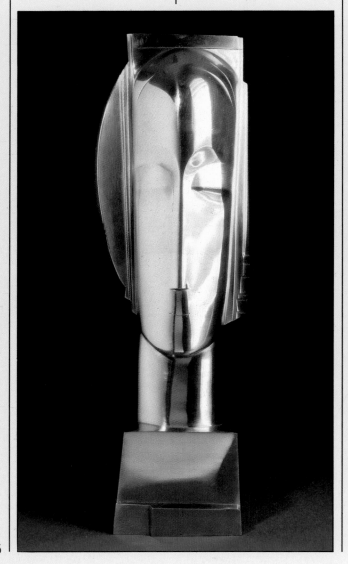

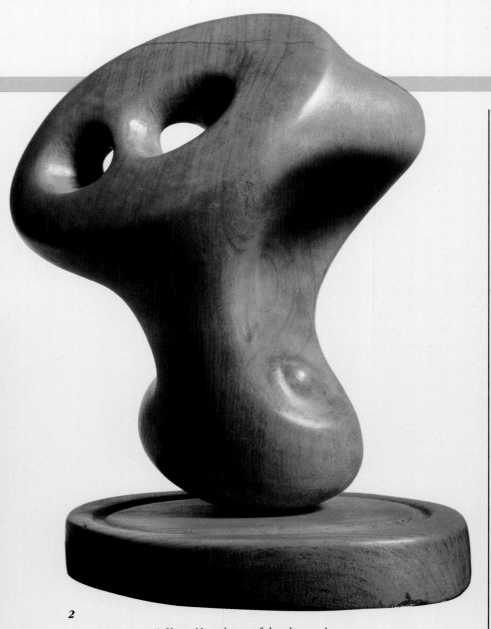

2

*Henry Moore's powerful and sensuous sculptures (**2**) owe more to natural forms and his reverence for the materials with which he worked than to intellectual abstractionism. The evident enjoyment of the qualities of the wood in* Composition *(1933) finds its echo in much of the non-commercial glass produced from the 1930s – by such figures as Maurice Marinot – to the present day.*

As the century has progressed, ceramics and glass have become increasingly abstract while painting interestingly moves in the opposite direction, towards representationalism. Gotlind Weigel's pots (**4**), called Stone Forms, made in 1990, emulate the qualities of stone both in their surface texture and simple, hewn shapes.

The posters of Cassandre (**5**) many of which were commissioned by the French railways and various shipping companies, marvellously express the feeling of speed and urgency that characterized the machine age. Streamlined, sleek forms, whether strictly necessary or not, caught the public imagination, as they seemed to epitomize efficiency and technological known-how.

3

Bernard Leach, who studied in Japan and integrated Japanese philosophies into his work (**3**), was a vastly influential figure, and remains so today twenty years after his death (he died in 1979).

4

5

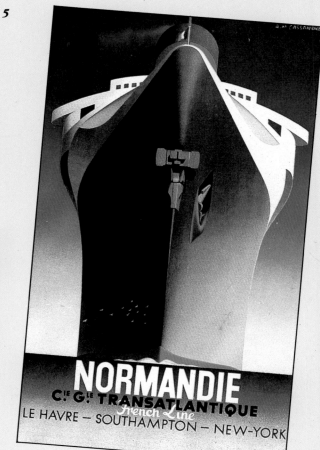

ART DECO

1 *Frederick Carder, head of Steuben Glass, designed this hexagonal vase in the 1920s, though its wavy floral motif is more reminiscent of the earlier organic Art Nouveau style. Note the grainy surface of different sized spots on the peacock-blue ground, like reverse condensation on the glass.*

1

2

3

3 *New Zealand-born architect Keith Murray began designing glass for Whitefriars and Stevens & Williams in the 1930s (he also created ceramic forms for Wedgwood). This thick-walled blue-green vase is a fine example of his classic forms, whose decoration was restrained, subtle and above all integral to the pieces.*

2 *The stylized blossoms and leaves, the chequerboard pattern on the rim, and the black, white and gold hues of this Quenvit footed bowl are all characteristic of the Art Deco style. The form was hand-painted with enamel paints.*

5

4 *The black-enamelled motifs and largely rectilinear shapes seen in and on this French liqueur set from the 1920s are pure Art Deco. Its maker is possibly Baccarat.*

5 *This overlaid- and etched-glass vase was designed by Josef Hoffmann and made by the Austrian firm Loetz Witwe. Its geometric designs are very much in the Art Deco vein, but its leaf-and-berry motif harks back to earlier, organic Arts and Crafts patterns. Many of Hoffmann's turn-of-the century Viennese designs were in fact harbingers of* moderne *things to come in France.*

4

EXPERIMENTAL GLASS

1 *Fauve painter turned studio-glassmaker Maurice Marinot single-handedly created some 2500 one-off vessels during his rich career as the premier glass artist in Art Deco France. This handsome bottle with stopper of 1925 has a burst of vari-sized air bubbles captured within its thick, clear-glass walls. Marinot expertly exploited what had once been considered flaws in glass – bubbles, streaks, etc. – and turned them into primary, decorative elements.*

2 *The rich, thick green glass of this flask with stopper of 1929, also by Marinot, is embellished both internally and externally: a smattering of black inclusions is captured within its coloured body, and acid etching adds a grainy texture that echoes the inner suspended pattern.*

3 *André Thuret, whose heavy glass vessels were influenced by the works of Marinot, created this candleholder with clear-glass "ears" and copper-coloured inclusions dating from 1945-55.*

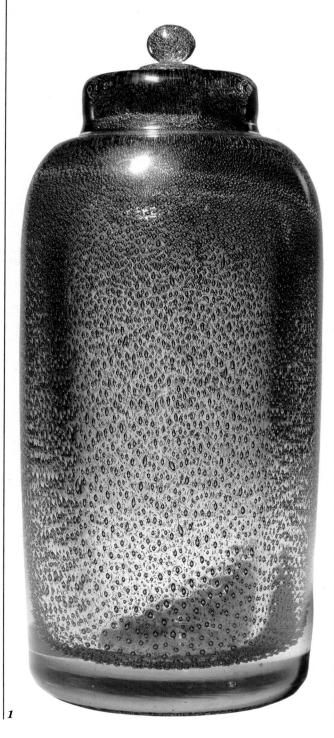

1

2

3

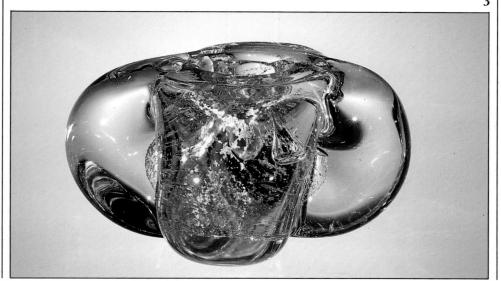

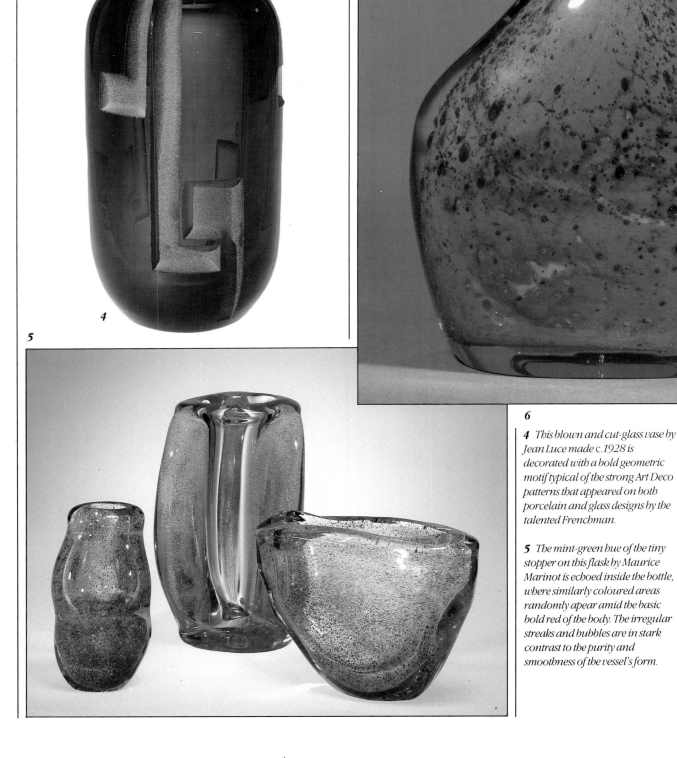

4 *This blown and cut-glass vase by Jean Luce made c.1928 is decorated with a bold geometric motif typical of the strong Art Deco patterns that appeared on both porcelain and glass designs by the talented Frenchman.*

5 *The mint-green hue of the tiny stopper on this flask by Maurice Marinot is echoed inside the bottle, where similarly coloured areas randomly apear amid the basic bold red of the body. The irregular streaks and bubbles are in stark contrast to the purity and smoothness of the vessel's form.*

6 *This trio of irregularly shaped blown-glass vases was created c.1945-55 by André Thuret, who was noted for his internally decorated (usually with coloured specks) pieces that he pinched and pulled into unusual, asymmetrical forms.*

PATE DE VERRE

1 Pâte de verre ("glass paste") is made by mixing together powdered glass with water and an adhesive medium, then applying it in a mould and firing it very carefully so as not to destroy the mould or cause the substance to fall apart. The technique was an ancient Egyptian one, revived by Henri Cros in late nineteenth century France. Among the major exponents were Alméric Walter, who created the fish-embellished plaque and bee-strewn dish here, and Gabriel Argy-Rousseau, maker of the alabaster-like vase and blue Bacchus mask- and leaf-decorated round box.

2

2 *Gabriel Argy-Rousseau produced* pâte de verre *glass decorated with flowers, animals and human figures. This vase is very much in the Art Deco vein, with its dark line of squares on the rim and base, its largely stylized blossoms and its lemon-yellow vertical sunrays set all round the ovoid form. The glassmaker studied ceramics at Sèvres before turning to a successful career in glass.*

3 *An elegant dancing Neoclassical figure adorns this Argy-Rousseau vase, whose alabaster-like qualities are clearly evident. Note the cloudy coloration and rough surface texture of the lower half of the vessel, and the clearer, smoother qualities of the upper panel and rim.*

3

LALIQUE BOTTLES

1

2

1 *The rich green hue of these two c. 1925 Lalique scent bottles is quite unusual in the French glassmaker's oeuvre. At left is* Le Jade, *created for Roger et Gallet and based on a Japanese snuff-bottle form, and at right is* Amélie, *with its layered petal or leaf shape terminating in a bud-like stopper. The latter bottle was sold empty by the Lalique firm and selected retailers, whereas* Le Jade *was sold filled with perfume, as is the practice today.*

2 *The flacon* Lunaria, *decorated with* monnaie-du-pape *pods, dates from around 1910 and is one of Lalique's early scent bottles.*

3 *The* Pan *flacon, c. 1912, is an outstanding example of a Neoclassical Lalique perfume container. Dramatic masks of the bearded and horned forest deity surround the bottle.*

3

4 Black-glass perfume bottles were not unusual in Lalique's production, although the Lézard flacon at left is quite rare. Ambre D'Orsay (right), was created for the parfumeur D'Orsay.

5 Among the Lalique flacons most sought after by present-day collectors are those of the large, overflowing-stopper variety. At left is Bouchon fleurs de pommier and at right is Bouchon mures; both c. 1929.

4

5

6 Lalique also designed several scent pendants, which could be suspended from a cord around the neck. At left is Sirènes, and on the right A Côtes Bouchon Papillon (as it is called in Lalique's 1932 catalogue).

7 This was one of Lalique's earliest designs for François Coty, made for his scent Ambre Antique in 1910.

6

7

SCULPTURAL

1

1 Voilée, Mains Jointes, c. *1920, is one of René Lalique's several full-length standing female figures. The clear-glass, diaphanous veil nicely surrounds the woman's face and gown which, in the proper light, glow with iridescence.*

2 *Lalique's frosted-glass statue, Grande Nue (Bras Levés), dates from c. 1920. The monumental figure, who is offering a gift to the gods, is not sculpted in the round, but seems to "emerge" from a tall block of glass behind her.*

3 *A one-off piece from the early twentieth century, this cire-perdue glass vase by Lalique was created by a casting method adapted from ancient bronzemaking, where the mould is destroyed in the process.*

2

3

4

4 *René Lalique produced a menagerie of creatures that were offered as automobile mascots in the 1920s and '30s. This rare example,* Hibou *(owl), dates from c. 1928.*

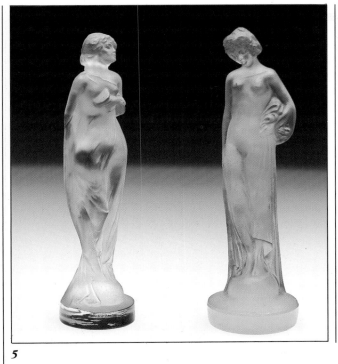

5 Moyenne Voilée *and* Moyenne Nue, *two c. 1920 Lalique figurines, present the modern French glass master's versions of Goya's naked and clothed* maja. *In fact, both women's bodies are fully covered, but their silhouetttes are somewhat erotically revealed.*

6 *Aristide Colotte's mask-like sculpture of c. 1931 seems to magically emerge from a jagged block of glass. Colotte is best known for his deeply carved or chiselled vessels and sculptures.*

7 *Glass – which has been cut, etched, engraved and leaded – is not the only component of this laminated mixed-media sculpture by American Susan Stinsmuehlen (b 1948). Whimsically entitled* Bacchante Texana, *it dates from 1985.*

5

6

7

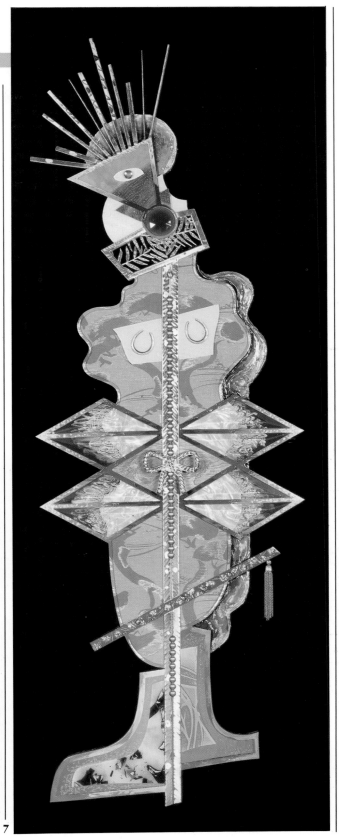

VASE FORMS

1 *American Mark Peiser's 1978 vase, Wisteria Trees PWV 079, has a magical, otherworldly quality. Its tall, smooth egg shape is like an elongated crystal ball, and the trees and blossoms, wholly occupying the form from base to lip, could be a vision of an ideal protected Eden.*

2 *René Lalique's bright blue Archers vase, c. 1922, has a classic ovoid form, its bulbous upper section moulded overall with large birds, its lower with muscular men aiming their bows. The vase was made in several colours.*

3 *A fierce Oriental-inspired dragon adorns this Dutch vase designed by De Lorm for the Leerdam factory, which was founded in 1765 and renowned in the twentieth century for its Art Nouveau and Art Deco glassware.*

3

2

4 *Timo Sarpaneva (b 1926), one of the Finnish glass factory Iittala's most important designers in this century, achieved great recognition, notably in the 1950s, for his highly sculptural vessels. This dramatic vase is called Charitas.*

5 *Like the blue Lalique vase on the previous page, this vessel, Aigrettes (c. 1922), also by Lalique, is decorated at the top with birds with dramatic, sweeping wing-spans. The egrets fly amid tall feathery grasses.*

6 *A frieze of etched birds against a geometric backdrop occupies the upper section of this white-cased and mottled-brown vase from the 1920s by Legras. Auguste Legras set up a glasshouse near Paris in St Denis in 1864, and the factory was noted for its Art Nouveau and Art Deco enamelled cameo glass.*

5

6

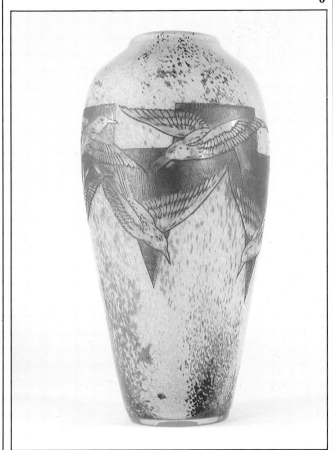

VASE FORMS

1

2

3

1 *The Swedish glass factory, Orrefors, produced this moulded-glass vase in the 1930s, to a design by Vicke Lindstrand, who worked at the firm from 1928 to 1941. The nude woman riding on a fish, wheel-engraved on the thick-walled glass, is typical of the stylized Art Deco figures that appeared on 1920s and '30s glass and ceramics – both in and* *outside France, the birthplace of the Art Deco style. The undulating rim and sides of the vase nicely complement the vessel's aquatic theme.*

2 *This mould-blown vase was designed by Eva Englund for Orrefors, and uses the Graal technique developed at the Swedish factory after the First World War to improve on the cased glass they already produced. Entitled* The Sea Maid, *it features a stylized mermaid swimming in a murky blue-green marine environment.*

4

3 The standard flask form has been transformed into a magical floriate wonderland on this overlaid-, carved-, etched- and enamelled-glass vase by Ludwig Moser & Sons of Karlsbad, a firm that continues to produce glass today. The vivid blue of the morning-glory blossom, with its thick, carved leaves, stands out in a largely monochromatic, but partly gilded, background of other flowers and fronds.

4 The fluid, expressive qualities of this assortment of postwar Italian glass are evident in the colours, shapes and decoration of the pieces. The chartreuse and black vase at left has snakeskin-like patterning, the tall vase next to it is pink lined with blue and the small round vase in the foreground has an abstract design overall, yet the forms of the three are smooth and regular. The cut-out vase and elliptical bowl, on the other hand, are irregularly shaped, and are examples of the 1950s enthusiasm for the uneven, undulating line.

TABLEWARE

1

2

3

1 This sextet of goblets made in 1978 by Massachusetts glass artist Josh Simpson and entitled New Mexico are of blown amethyst-tinted glass with blue-grey decoration and clear stems. The rich, internally decorated pattern on the bowls was inspired by the dramatic landscape of the American state, hence the name of the glasses.

2 The handsome footed bowl with its engraved design of a trapeze artist/balancing act was designed by Russian-born artist Pavel Tchelitchev for Steuben Glass. From 1940 Steuben's director of design, John Monteith Gates, commissioned twenty-seven designs by Tchelitchev and other well-known artists, including Henri Matisse, Georgia O'Keeffe, Jean Cocteau and Eric Gill.

3 The Dane Jesper Kerrn-Jespersen created this set of four blown "snapglasses" with multicoloured reed-like inclusions. They date from 1977.

4 *The wide variety of shapes and colours in drinking glasses available in the early twentieth century is clearly demonstrated by these ten examples. Wiener Werkstätte designer Otto Prutscher created the mauve, yellow and blue goblets with geometric cameo-cut stems for the firm Meyr's Neffe. Other designs and factories represented are Karl Koepping, Karl Massanetz, Theresienthal & Josephinhutte, and J. & L. Lobmeyr.*

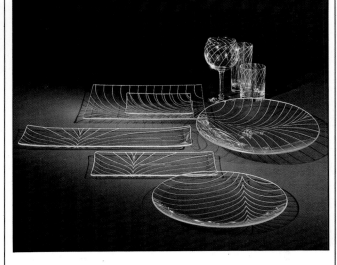

5 *The simple, folk-art-inspired floral motifs on these four drinking glasses, designed by Eva Englund and made by Orrefors in 1983-84, are offset by the vessels' rather sophisticated shapes. They are from the Maja tableware service.*

6 *William J. Kolano of Irene Pasinski Associates created the handsome components of the Designer Collection, Windswept Pattern for the Susquehanna Glass Company. Dating from 1977, they feature subtle patterns of kinetic wheel-cut lines.*

ABSTRACT

1 Dating from 1983, Robert Willson's torso-shaped glass sculpture is a red, white, blue and gold-flecked enigma – at once a crucifix, a face and an abstract exercise in a variety of techniques. It is largely in the thick-walled, internally decorated style originated by Marinot in the 1920s and continued in the American Studio Craft Movement, which began in the 1960s.

1

2 American Ginny Ruffner's abstract glass sculpture, Eat Your Hat, dates from 1985. The flameworked, candy-coloured concoction is enhanced with paint and pastels, and comprises dozens of attached shapes on three "legs" that support a four-limbed central segment.

2

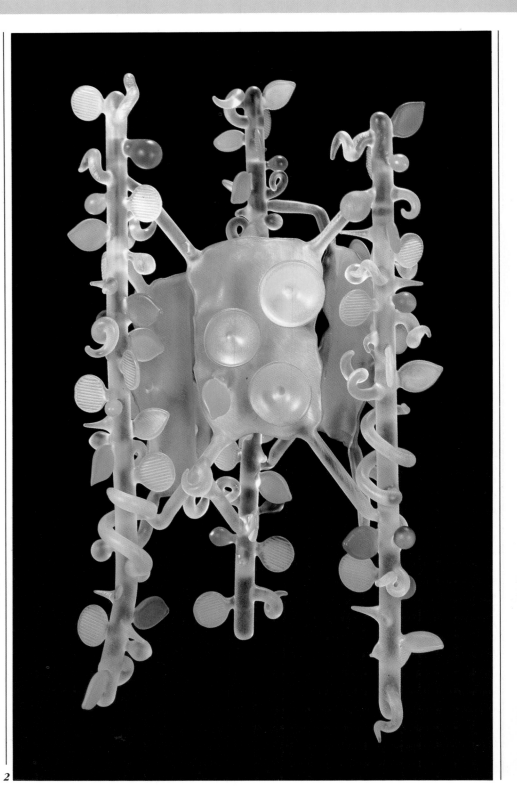

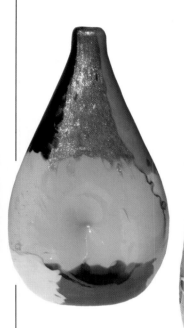

3

4

5

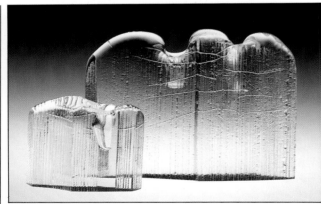

6

3 *The dominant turquoise, yellow and gold of these two Post-war, internally decorated Italian vases are common colours in 1950s glass. The example at left is an Aureliano Toso "Oriente" pezzato vetri vase, with internally fused segments resembling a patchwork.*

4 *Oiva Toikka designed this whimsical glass sculpture, Lollipop Isle, in 1969. Of both moulded and free-blown glass in joyously vivid colours, it is an early example of a favourite theme of this artist, whose latter works are even more daring.*

5 *Ettore Sottsass, a leading figure of the Milan-based design group, Memphis, designed this colourful fruit bowl called Sol in 1982.*

6 *These two sculptural vases are by the gifted Finnish designer Tapio Wirkkala and were made by the Iittala glassworks. Of clear colourless glass, they date from 1955 and are simply called* Paaders, *which means ice blocks. Wirkkala has been associated with Iittala since 1947, but is a versatile artist-craftsman who also works in wood and silver.*

MODERN FORMS

1 American glassmaker Dale Chihuly constantly experiments with a wide variety of forms and techniques. This delicate multipart sculpture of thin-walled, shell-like nesting forms is entitled Davy's Gray Sea Form with Black Lip Wraps. It was made in 1985 by Chihuly with Kate Elliott and other glassblowers, probably at Pilchuck Center.

2 Romanian glass artist Dan Bancila created this handsome tripartite sculpture, Blue Shapes, in 1978. Of colourless and cobalt-blue glass, the blown pieces have been cut and acid-etched.

3 The inherent irregularity of many modern glass vessels, such as these three pieces, results in glass sculpture whose emphasis is on technique and decoration, with form a second consideration dictated by the method used. The conical vase in the middle is by Venini, while the other two pieces are by AVEM.

4 *This impressive covered bowl dates from the 1930s and is engraved with a pattern of large squares alternating with small crosses. It is by Edvard Strömberg* *(1872-1946), a talented Swedish glass designer and technician who worked for the Kosta, Orrefors and Eda glassworks before starting up his own factory in 1933.*

4

6

5 *The swirling red and yellow pattern on this low bowl, with its central black bull's-eye, was achieved by encasing the colours in a layer of clear glass. It was made by Anthony Stern in 1983.*

6 *This freely formed, thick-walled glass vase in yellowish-green opalescent glass has a satisfying sculptural quality. It was made at the University of Wisconsin by Harvey K. Littleton in 1965.*

CREDITS

Quarto would like to thank the following for their help with this publication and for permission to reproduce copyright material.

ABBREVIATIONS USED:

Bridgeman = Bridgeman Art Library: BM = By Courtesy of the Trustees of the British Museum: Christie's = Christie's Colour Library: Corning = Corning Museum of Glass, Corning, New York. Phillips = Phillips Fine Art Auctioneers: RGM = Romisch-Germanisches Museum: Sotheby's = Sotheby's Auctioneers, London. V & A = By Courtesy of the Board and Trustees of the Victoria & Albert Museum